Resonance of Democracy

UNRAVELLING THE TAPESTRY OF TELANGANA ELECTIONS 2023

PALWAI RAGHAVENDRA REDDY

TAKSHAŚILA MUDRANA

ISBN: 978-81-970534-1-2
First published 2024

Published by

TAKSHAŚILA MUDRANA

Imprint of Parjanya Consultants Private Limited
Hyderabad, INDIA
www.takshasilamudrana.com
contact@takshasilamudrana.com
Printed in India by Maruthi Graphics, Hyderabad

Mom . Dad . S4

Resonance of Democracy

Contents

Resonance of Democracy

Foreword

Nearly 75 days after the Telangana State Assembly Elections, this book, authored by Palwai Raghavendra Reddy (popularly known as Raghav), unravels the political quicksand of the relatively new state of Telangana. Aptly titled *'Resonance of Democracy: Unravelling the Tapestry of Telangana Elections 2023'*, the book reasons out how the then incumbent Bharat Rashtra Samithi (BRS) government completely missed out in reading the writing on the wall, despite its flagship welfare schemes.

The author rightly states that these elections were "more than a mere political event, they are a reflection of the collective aspirations of a people, a state at a crossroads. The characters in this narrative are not merely politicians; they are architects of change, custodians of public trust, and embodiments of the hopes and dreams of millions".

The book vividly captures the essence of this democratic process through the very first chapter *'Byelections & Munugode'* and sets the stage with detailed reporting on how the decisive victory of the grand old Congress party in Karnataka boosted the local Congress party's confidence in taking on KCR, the patriarch of Telangana. Another chapter titled *'Turncoats & Tickets'* delves deep into how political parties across ideological lines made desperate attempts to attract 'turncoats' in order to get to the wheels of power and how they accommodated them by giving tickets looking only at the winnability factor.

The phenomenon of the firebrand Revanth Reddy and the way he mobilised youth by focusing on two important areas, education and employment, is elegantly explained. The articulation of their frustrations, pitched as a campaign strategy, brought the youth back into the Congress fold. This realignment has been treated well by Raghav in his own, inimitable style of writing. It is pertinent to state here that good writers run through numerous drafts to come up with riveting prose and it takes years of writing to master the narrative. That the author has made such an attempt itself is a testimony to the fact that he'll emerge as an arresting writer in the days to come.
Raghav has been in the thick of political communication. Along with his friends Nitin Tanksale, Sreekar Reddy, and Pavan Nanduri, he designed, developed, and participated in political campaigns for political parties and individuals since 2009 across Telangana, Odisha, Chhattisgarh, and Andhra Pradesh. Supported by the rigour of field research, especially one-on-one interviews done across the length and breadth of Telangana, the book provides insights into the reasons for change. The campaign trail, the media blitzkrieg of both BRS and Congress coupled with 'acceptable' narratives, especially the Indir-amma guarantees, caught the imagination of the people in Telangana.

The book also narrates how the father and son duo, Kalvakuntla Chandrashekar Rao and Kalvakuntla Taraka Rama Rao (KCR & KTR for short), made a desperate attempt to attract voters and how the final blow to the BRS citadel was delivered by the people, who were waiting for change. The resurgence of the Congress Party, the limited influence of Narendra Modi and the BJP, and the open alignment of Owaisi brothers with the ruling BRS dispensation led many Muslims to realign and vote for the Congress Party, as they saw a new beacon of hope in Revanth Reddy, despite his RSS leanings in early life.

Raghav further goes on to paint a realistic picture of Revanth Reddy and how the tacit support of N Chandra Babu Naidu and the Seemandhra people with their sizeable presence in most constituencies made a difference in bringing about the change in Telangana. How all such factors led to the victory of the Congress Party, how a strong contingent of young, alert voters were instrumental in ushering in the change through a decisive verdict forms the heart of this story. Raghav also analyses the ongoing tussle in the assembly and what it points to in the future. In a nutshell, Resonance of Democracy shows that "when power goes to the head, heads simply roll." Raghav with his first book succinctly expresses this truth.

Prof. Karnam Narender
Former Dean, Faculty of Social Sciences Social Sciences,
Senior Professor, Department of Communication and Journalism
University College of Arts & Social Sciences,
Osmania University, Hyderabad

Preface

We live in a divided world. There are too many opinions and too few facts. Switch on the television and you will hear pundits spewing out opinions. Self-anointed experts on social media toss around yet more opinions. Amid all this noise, we forget that opinions are not facts. We argue over the former and pay scant attention to the latter.

The author of this book has always prized facts over opinions. A professional sceptic, he takes no one's opinions at face value–not even his own. His reading, which is prodigious, is unbiased and he seeks out conversations with people who hold diverse viewpoints. Sometimes, these are fellow political observers. Most often, they are farmers, students and all manner of commonfolk he runs into. As he notes at the start, the germ of this book was a conversation he had with a group of farmers in the Telangana hinterland. In the pages that follow, he takes us through an engaging, fact-based tour of the Telangana State Assembly Elections 2023. If you pay attention, you will hear the muffled roar of democracy.

I hasten to add that political facts do not have the same standing as scientific facts. Water boils at 100°C – a verifiable fact. In politics, by contrast, such hard facts are elusive, which is one reason why we are so divided. The emergence of social media has further hardened our divisions. Times were good when the late US politician Daniel Patrick Moynihan quipped that "everyone is entitled to his own opinion, but not his own facts". Today, whether we like it or not, people have their own facts and they use them to beat up others.

These "alternative facts" make it difficult to attain a clear understanding of our politics.

One admirable aspect of this book is the author's ability to employ commonly-agreed facts whenever they exist. When there aren't any, he painstakingly presents diverse and often contrasting perspectives to bring a nuanced picture into sharp focus. Independent assertions may not always be factual, but an objective compilation of these holds greater validity than gossip. Take for example the elections this book covers. What enabled the Telangana Congress to upset the Bharat Rashtra Samithi, which looked invincible months before the election? If you read media reportage, you will be forgiven for thinking that Fake News and Arrogance got in the ring. Final tally: Fake News 1. Arrogance 0.

Such simplistic reasoning does not explain a truly divided result. This book shows how the result expressed the divergent fortunes experienced by different groups of people over the last 10 years. Like it is said of some places, Telangana has more history than geography. This small state has witnessed hyperactive political manoeuvring, thanks to the presence of charismatic, shrewd and ambitious political leaders in the fray. The result, therefore, cannot turn on one or two things. This is exactly why we need a comprehensive and clear-headed account of the winds that converged to create the perfect storm on November 30, 2023. The book in your hands answers this need, artfully integrating the story of these elections into the larger story of democracy.

The author's deep understanding of Telangana and its politics shines through on every page. Of the several insights that line its pages, I want to pick two here. The first is that Telangana politics is as much a contest of personalities as it is of policies. The character and values of leaders matter significantly in forming voting preferences. Therefore, narrating the story of these elections through vignettes of the key people makes for an excellent choice. We know the prime movers and what moves them.

The second insight is the normalisation of welfare. People take welfare policies for granted. No party can, the popular reasoning goes, scale back welfare policies and invite voter wrath. This could have far-reaching implications. These expectations will lead to increased welfare spending that will have to someday crash into the stone wall of economic reality. More of one thing is less of something else. That's Economics 101. We can kick the can down the road, but for only so long. What comes after this welfare spring?

The book's refreshingly balanced and inquiring tone makes the reader smart in a way that ordinary political reporting does not. With the author as your guide, you learn how KCR imperiously ignored the unfavourable findings of a survey conducted by the author's colleague. He takes you into the psyche of people who felt offended by KTR's reaction to the arrest of N Chandrababu Naidu. An anecdote from 2014 shows how a swift-footed Harish Rao greenlighted a unique campaign initiative in Sircilla just five minutes into the pitch. Elsewhere, he explains how fierce ambition fuelled Revanth Reddy's rise and how he was helped by Congress's victory in Karnataka. The author isn't given to descriptive excesses, so there won't be any descriptions of Alair chai or chapter-length commentaries on Cheriyal scroll paintings.

This book is all about politics and what it means for the future of Telangana.

Let's get into the story now. After you have finished reading, if you find yourself remarking that this is one of the most perceptive commentaries ever written on Telangana politics, be so kind as to remember who said it first.

Shashi Polavarapu
24-02-2024

Introduction

Over the years, I travelled to various parts of Telangana as part of my professional engagement. During one such journey in September 2022, I had an interesting discussion with a group of farmers at Ramreddypally village in Thimmajipet mandal of Nagarkurnool district, about 130 km south of Hyderabad. Seeing a group of six farmers aged between the late 40s and 70s, my colleagues and I stopped to understand their political acumen and leaning. All six farmers belonged to the 'most' backward class of our society, and none held more than two acres of land (at least three of these six distributed the land among their children). While all of their families received Rythu Bandhu, at least four out of the six in this group are beneficiaries of the State government's old-age pensions.

We introduced ourselves as independent journalists travelling in the region to assess people's mood one year before Telangana State goes for elections. Mallaiah, the youngest in the group, was sympathetic towards the ruling Telangana Rashtra Samithi (before it was renamed Bharat Rashtra Samithi on October 5, 2022) because he was a beneficiary of the Rythu Bandhu scheme. While Mallaiah was close to the village sarpanch, who belonged to the party in power, others had no connections with any political party.

We received interesting responses when we asked them what the general mood in the region was and who they thought would win if elections were held in the State immediately. These individuals said Telangana Rashtra Samithi and Chief Minister Kalvakuntla Chandrashekhar Rao are still in the pole position, but they weren't sure what will happen in the next twelve months. When asked about the Indian National Congress (INC or Congress party), they said its leaders are busy fighting among themselves and not sure if they would put up a spirited fight against the incumbent. Speaking about the Bharatiya Janata Party (BJP), they said they hear much in the media about the saffron party, Prime Minister Narendra Modi and State party president Bandi Sanjay. However, none from that political outfit is visible on the ground.

Curious about his observations, I interjected, "What factors would influence their vote in the Assembly polls?"

Though others were non-committal about what would influence their decision, Mallaiah stated that pensions would play a significant role. "Many people, such as the elderly, widows, and people with a physical disability, are getting pensions from the government. They will be grateful to the Chief Minister when they vote."

Rangaiah, a septuagenarian and possibly the oldest in that group of six farmers, jumped in to negate his earlier statement. Rangaiah disagreed with his younger farmer and said welfare schemes would continue, and poor people would get pensions irrespective of the party in power.
He confidently stated that no one can stop these welfare schemes now and specifically mentioned, "If one party announces Rs 2000 as a pension, another will better it to

Rs 3000, but no one will stop it."

Rangaiah's argument was an eye-opener for me, especially after coming across a different mood during the Telangana State Assembly elections in 2018.

In 2018, many farmers who held less than or more than five acres of cultivable land and were getting Rythu Bandhu were apprehensive of this scheme continuing at the same scale if the TRS loses the election. Many beneficiaries of various pension schemes worried that the amount they were receiving would be revised backwards. Such apprehensions and multiple other political factors resulted in a big win for KCR and his party. But now, the winds of change seemed to be blowing.

This episode at Ramreddypally and many such interactions with commoners across the State prompted me to capture the mood and the verdict Telangana delivered on November 30, 2023.

This book *'Resonance of Democracy: Unraveling the Tapestry of Telangana Elections 2023'* is an outcome of my interactions with voters over 15 months and my observations of political manoeuvres executed by political leaders. Whether meeting a group of women farmers in Gadwal district, or meeting a bunch of roadside hawkers in Khammam, or interacting with few traders in Nalgonda, or learning about the lives of farmers in Karimnagar, or speaking to the students of Osmania University in Hyderabad, each of these interactions enriched me with more significant and deeper understanding of the Telangana State.

In 2018, many thought there was a certain degree of anti-incumbency in the State, but in the end, the Telangana Rashtra Samithi returned to power with an enhanced mandate. In 2023, I had to tour more regions, visit more villages, and speak to many more people before assessing in which direction Telangana voters would lean. One such experience came my way when I read a brief news article, *"Protest erupts in Gajwel as many fail to get Dalit Bandhu benefits"*, in the *Deccan Chronicle* on August 13, 2023.

This headline caught my attention, and the very next day, I visited Teegul village in Jagdevpur Mandal, which is a part of KCR's Gajwel Constituency, to understand the situation on the ground. While interacting with the villagers, I noticed that quite a few Dalit families were demanding housing and financial support under the Dalit Bandhu scheme. However, there was no immediate way to verify if these villagers were eligible to get benefits under these two schemes, the most prominent welfare schemes introduced by the TRS (rechristened as BRS by then) government. I noticed significant dissatisfaction among these villagers over not receiving benefits under these two schemes.

Stopping our car randomly and, at times, inadvertently, we interacted with farmers, students, employees, men, women, old and young, to understand what factors influence them. Despite hundreds of attempts, we could not see a clear trend or a wave coming in the elections. However, a direction was sometimes visible in one region, but the next area used to throw up a different dimension. Overall, it was a fantastic experience.

Though my friends Nitin Tanksale, Sreekar Reddy, and Pavan Nanduri and I designed, developed, and participated in political campaigns for political parties and individuals since 2009 across Telangana, Odisha, Chhattisgarh, and Andhra Pradesh, the 2023 Telangana State Assembly elections changed me and my friends.

These elections were more than a mere political event, they were a reflection of the collective aspirations of a people. The characters in this book are not merely politicians, but they are architects of change, and embodiments of the hopes and dreams of millions.

I have written hundreds of short drafts and articles, but this is my first-ever attempt at book-writing. I sincerely hope the reader will encourage my first attempt, and in the process, I hope I get motivated to write more in the times ahead.

Byelections & Munugode

In the Indian political landscape, Chanakya is considered India's topmost strategist - Machaveli. However, even Chanakya had to draft Chandragupta to implement his ideas. One may find many examples of Chanakya, the brain, and Chandragupta, the body. Kalvakuntla Chandrashekhar Rao (KCR), however, is one of the few exceptions as he was the brain and body that ran the agitation demanding Statehood for the Telangana region. He won the first elections of Telangana state and kept it under his tight control.

In 2018, however, he surprised his political opponents and the people of Telangana by dissolving the State Assembly nine months ahead of its term. With no crisis or political instability, KCR's decision baffled everyone. Though his political opponents raked up issues like corruption and his family's larger-than-expected footprint in the government, they failed to convince the people of Telangana. The TRS returned to power with an even greater mandate.

While the ruling Telangana Rashtra Samithi won 88 seats, a sharp increase of 25 seats from 2014, the main opposition, the Congress party, lost two seats compared to earlier elections and stood at 19. The All India Majlis-e-Ittehadul Muslimeen (AIMIM) of the Owaisi Brothers, an unofficial ally of the ruling party, retained the same seven seats it won in 2014. Once a prominent force in the Telangana region, the Telugu Desam Party (TDP) lost its relevance in the State by 2018 and shrunk to just two seats from the 15 it won in 2014.

From 2012-13, then Chief Minister of Gujarat and later the Prime Minister of India, Narendra Modi, was at the centre of politics in India. In 2014, the Bharatiya Janata Party allied with the Telugu Desam Party in Telangana and Andhra Pradesh. While the BJP won five seats in Telangana in addition to the TDP's 15, this alliance came into power in Andhra Pradesh in 2014. However, the political puzzle in Andhra Pradesh led to the TDP severing its ties with the BJP. The BJP went into polls without any alliance partners in Telangana first and later in Andhra Pradesh.

The Bharatiya Janata Party, which held five seats in Telangana in 2014, all coming from Hyderabad city limits, was reduced to just one seat in the 2018 elections. Big names like then State unit chief Dr K Laxman, Gangapuram Kishan Reddy, N.V.S.S. Prabhakar, and Chintala Ramchandra Reddy lost their respective seats. Thakur Raja Singh Lodh, aka T. Raja Singh, was the lone victor among BJP contestants. Raja Singh retained his Goshamahal seat with a decent margin of 17,734 votes over his rival Prem Singh Rathore of the TRS.

Such a disastrous result would have disheartened any political party. But the BJP is different. It always keeps looking for opportunities to expand into new territories.

One such opportunity came the BJP's way when Solipeta Ramalinga Reddy, a TRS legislator from the Dubbak Assembly Constituency, passed away in August 2020. For several decades, a practice evolved in Telangana that allowed the election of the deceased's kin unopposed. The BJP ignored the precedent of the old establishment and entered the fray in the bypolls held in November 2020.

The BJP fielded Madhavaneni Raghunandan Rao, a rebel TRS leader and a close relative of KCR, in Dubbak. Raghunandan Rao had contested from Dubbak in 2018 and 2014 and finished as a distant third. The TRS fielded Solipeta Sujatha Reddy, the widow of Solipeta Ramalinga Reddy. T. Harish Rao, one of the most high-profile ministers and KCR's nephew, was given charge of the byelection.

The campaign that followed will remain a classic in Telangana history. While the TRS had power and money, Raghunandan Rao did not have either. Surprisingly, neither KCR nor Amit Shah turned up to support their respective candidates. The result was a surprise. The BJP's Raghunandan Rao defeated his TRS rival, who had power, money and sympathy. But the margin was slender – just 1,079 votes. Raghunandan Rao polled 63,352 votes, the TRS candidate got 62,273 votes, and the Congress party got just 13.5 per cent of total votes. This win gave a new lease of life to the saffron brigade in Telangana, and the party had their second legislator in the Assembly. The celebrations that followed this win indicated that the BJP was not out of the race for power in this State. The party felt that the victory in bypolls could be a template to establish itself as a primary challenger to the TRS.

On December 1, 2020, Nagarjuna Sagar legislator Nomula Narasimhaiah passed away. It led to a bypoll in May 2021 to elect a new MLA from the Nagarjuna Sagar Assembly Constituency. The BJP tried replicating its Dubbak model but failed as the ruling Telangana Rashtra Samithi retained the seat. The ruling party's Nomula Bhagat, son of the late Nomula Narasimhaiah, defeated the Congress party warhorse Kunduru Jana Reddy with a comfortable margin of 18,872 votes. It was the second successive defeat for Jana Reddy, whom Narasimhaiah beat in the 2018 State Assembly elections with a margin of 7,771 votes. BJP candidate P. Ravi Kumar Naik polled just four per cent or 7,676 votes. Having lost two elections from his constituency within three years, Jana Reddy retired from electoral politics, preferring to field his son Kunduru Jayaveer.

Its chequered progress in Telangana didn't dishearten the BJP, as the internal politics of the TRS provided it an excellent opportunity to expand its base.

Etela Rajender, Telangana State's first finance minister and a trusted KCR lieutenant, fell out with the party boss in 2021. The showdown between KCR and Etela began in April and May 2021, when the latter was accused of infringing on the land of some farmers in Achampet and Hakimpet villages in Medak district, where he ran a large hatchery, Jamuna Hatcheries, named after his wife Jamuna Reddy.

When the complaints surfaced against his minister, KCR stripped Etela of his ministerial portfolio and dropped him from the Cabinet a few days later. Following the dismissal, Etela Rajender resigned from the party on June 4, 2021, and his Assembly membership on June 12, necessitating a bypoll in Huzurabad.

Etela Rajender commanded tremendous goodwill in his constituency and was a well-known leader in the State. He got invitations from both the Congress party and the BJP. Revanth Reddy, the Telangana Pradesh Congress Committee chief, tried his best to persuade Etela to join the Congress party, but the latter chose to join the party in power in New Delhi.

Run by the Narendra Modi and Amit Shah brand of politics, the new-age BJP was ready to induct anyone, especially existing legislators or members of Parliament if they wished to shift their loyalty towards it. It needed more opportunities to keep the winning tempo until the next Assembly polls. On the other hand, Etela had his reasons for choosing the party in power at the Centre.

Even before quitting the party, Etela had tried to claim the legacy of the Telangana agitation and said that he was one of the owners of the TRS. This attempt made KCR concentrate all his energy on winning this seat and sending out a message on who owns the legacy of Telangana agitation.

The TRS attracted Padi Kaushik Reddy, a former cricketer and a Congress party candidate from Huzurabad in the 2018 elections. He polled 35 per cent of the votes. Initially, the TRS considered fielding Kaushik Reddy, but it changed the plan as it feared it would allow Etela to play his OBC card to the hilt. It fielded Gellu Srinivas Yadav, also from Backward Class but a non-local for Huzurabad.

The BJP, on the other hand, pooled all its resources to support Etela, who could put up an intense fight in his home constituency. Aware of the fact that Padi Kaushik Reddy took away the Congress party vote bank, the Congress party fielded the 29-year-old NSUI State unit president Balmoor Venkat Narsing Rao, a qualified doctor, from the seat. While many local leaders showed interest, Revanth Reddy-led TPCC decided on fielding a non-local for Huzurabad.

This byelection seemed like a personal battle between KCR and Etela Rajender. To attract many Scheduled Caste voters in the Huzurabad region, KCR announced the most ambitious scheme ever in Indian politics – the Dalit Bandhu scheme.

The Dalit Bandhu, announced in August 2021 as a pilot in Huzurabad, is an ambitious initiative launched by the State government to promote the economic development of families belonging to the SC community in Telangana. This scheme promised financial assistance of Rs 10 lakhs to eligible SC families, which they could use to start a business. At the launch of this scheme, the Chief Minister stated that this initiative is an affirmative action to help the marginalised sections of our society to become self-reliant and improve their standard of living. However, the Dalit Bandhu did not help the TRS win the Huzurabad byelection. In hindsight, this scheme damaged the KCR government's reelection prospects in the 2023 State Assembly elections.

Despite an all-out effort of the TRS government, the Huzurabad electorate resoundingly voted for Etela, who got a 52 per cent share of the votes. TRS candidate Gellu Srinivas Yadav, who got 40 per cent votes, lost the crucial poll by 23,855 votes. The Congress party was left red-faced as its vote shrunk from 34.6 per cent in 2018 to just 1.46 per cent in 2021. TPCC chief Revanth Reddy owned up responsibility for the debacle.

It was a festival mood at the Shyamaprasad Mookherjee Bhavan at Nampally in Hyderabad. Though the BJP's MLA count just reached three, the party now appeared as the main opposition to the ruling TRS in Telangana. The Congress party, people felt, would struggle to retain its main opposition party status in the State Assembly after the 2023 Assembly elections.

The BJP's spectacular performance in the 2020 Greater Hyderabad Municipal Corporation elections also contributed to its narrative. Union home minister and the party strongman Amit Shah and BJP national president J.P. Nadda campaigned extensively in Hyderabad for the GHMC election. Prime Minister Narendra Modi found a surrogate means to campaign for the party by visiting a Covid vaccine facility in Hyderabad. Just before the GHMC elections, Hyderabad bore the brunt of bad monsoon floods. Several colonies were inundated, and the TRS had mismanaged flood relief distribution. The result was obvious. The TRS tally fell to 56, nine less than its 2016 count. The BJP won 48 corporator segments as compared to just four in 2016. In terms of vote share, the TRS polled 1,204,167 or 35.81 per cent, and the BJP garnered 1,195,711 or 35.56 per cent. While the Congress party retained its tally of two seats, its vote share shrunk from almost 11 per cent in 2016 to just 6.68 per cent in 2020. Though the TRS captured the Mayor's post with the support of the AIMIM, the BJP established itself as a force in Hyderabad and Telangana.

With positive results in two out of three byelections and the

GHMC elections, the Bharatiya Janata Party attracted leaders and cadres from other political parties across Telangana. Many leaders from the Congress party and the Telugu Desam shifted to the BJP in Hyderabad and a few in districts. A few notable names include D.K. Aruna, Nagam Janardhan Reddy, and Jitender Reddy, among others.

The BJP turned impatient to strike the final blow, establishing the party as the favourite in the 2023 State Assemblyelections. It began discussions with many prominent leaders with an open invite to join the party. It wanted to set the narrative of a rising BJP through the bypoll template.

While most MLAs were not ready to risk their Assembly membership to join the BJP, Congress party MLA Komatireddy Rajgopal Reddy from the Munugode Constituency of Nalgonda district was ready for the gambit.

In August 2022, he quit his MLA post, complaining about the lack of development in the Munugode Constituency and blaming Chief Minister KCR for apathy towards seats represented by MLAs from opposition parties. When asked why he opted to join the BJP, Rajgopal Reddy said the TPCC was run by a "blackmailer" – accusing Revanth Reddy – who previously made derogatory remarks against Sonia Gandhi. While Revanth Reddy did not react to Rajgopal Reddy's statement, the party condemned his statement, and said that he quit the Congress party, and joined the BJP to protest his business interests.

Rajgopal Reddy's resignation forced another byelection in

Telangana and another opportunity for the BJP to strike gold. Leaders and cadres of all political parties watched the developments in Munugode with great interest as its result would set the tone for the 2023 State Assembly elections.

The BJP fielded Rajgopal Reddy, while the TRS opted for Kusukuntla Prabhakar Reddy, who fought from the seat in 2014 and 2018, winning once and losing the next time. The Congress party, which held this seat, fielded Palvai Sravanthi, the daughter of late Palvai Goverdhan Reddy, five times MLA from Munugode, who later became a member of the Rajya Sabha.

While Prabhakar Reddy had the ruling party's backing, Rajgopal Reddy was a financially sound candidate with the entire BJP might behind him. In comparison, the Congress party candidate was considered a lightweight.

The Munugode byelection, held in November 2022, generated maximum interest not just among the people of Telangana but also among political enthusiasts from around the country. Considered the most expensive election ever fought in the history of India, money was used to purchase loyalties and votes from the people. The TRS stationed ministers and MLAs at almost every village across Munugode, and money was pumped in large stashes.

According to Dubbak legislator Raghunandan Rao, the BJP spent Rs 100 crores in Munugode. On the polling day, Munugode voters claimed to have received at least Rs 3,000 per vote from the BJP camp and at least Rs 4,000 per vote from the TRS camp. Speaking to YouTubers and journalists,

The Karnataka Factor

Karnataka is the gateway to southern India for the Bharatiya Janata Party (BJP). While Uttar Pradesh and Yogi Adityanath are seen as the symbols of the rise of Hindutva in India, many in this south Indian State feel Karnataka is the "laboratory" for Hindutva politics. BJP leaders repeatedly stated that Telangana will be the second State in south India after Karnataka, where the saffron party will emerge victorious. After the mess the BJP got into in Munugode, the party needed a big win in the Karnataka State Assembly elections to influence Telangana voters and capture power in the second southern state.

The Bharatiya Janata Party (BJP) was in a peculiar situation ahead of the State Assembly elections in Karnataka. In the 2018 elections, the electorate had delivered a split verdict. The BJP was the largest party but did not command a majority in the Assembly. As the leader of the largest political party, B.S. Yediyurappa got an invitation from Governor Vajubhai Vala to form the government. However, the post-poll alliance between the Congress party and the Janata Dal (Secular) ensured that he did not get the support of the required legislators to prove his majority. Yediyurappa resigned, and H.D. Kumaraswamy, son of former Prime Minister H.D. Deve Gowda, was appointed the Chief Minister.

A year later, in June 2019, the BJP initiated "Operation Kamal", which toppled the Congress-JD(S) government. BJP strongman Yediyurappa was back as the Chief Minister on

July 26, 2019 – his fourth and possibly last term in the post. Exactly two years later, Yediyurappa reluctantly resigned from the post because of the BJP central leadership's desire to effect a generational change in the party, and his protégé Basavaraj Bommai became the Chief Minister. Basavaraj was from a political family in the State as his father, Somappa Rayappa Bommai, was the fourth Chief Minister of Karnataka.

Basavaraj Bommai, however, had a tough time in office. He faced severe backlash from the people of Karnataka on corruption charges. The Congress party's innovative campaign called Bommai "PayCM", a spoof alluding to PayTM and his government as the "40% Sarkara", struck a chord with the people. While the BJP banked heavily on Prime Minister Narendra Modi's popularity even in the State Assembly election, the Congress party ran an effective localised campaign.

A bit about the BJP's entry into Karnataka: Thanks to an extensive network laid by the RSS and its affiliates in the South Kanara region (Dakshina Kannada) since 1940, the BJP won 18 seats in the Karnataka State Assembly elections in 1983. Though 71 candidates lost their deposits, the 1983 election laid a strong foundation for the party in the years to come. In the initial years, most Brahmins and Jains extended unwavering support to the BJP. While this number was insufficient, it formed a strong core support base that ensured that the BJP was not an insignificant player in the state.

The Congress party's decision to remove Veerendra Patil, a prominent Lingayat face in the state, from the post of Chief

Minister in less than a year of assuming the office irked his community. According to numerous news reports and opinion articles published over the past three decades, the Lingayat community is yet to forgive India's grand old party for its 1990 decision.

It was at this time that the Bharatiya Janata Party started grooming Lingayat leadership within the party's rank and file, especially in the form of Bookanakere Siddalingappa Yediyurappa, popularly known as B.S. Yediyurappa, who went on to become the longest-serving BJP Chief Minister in Karnataka.

The rout of the Congress party in the 1994 elections with a 16.55 per cent negative swing in vote share allowed the BJP to emerge as the largest opposition party, having six more legislators than the Congress party. Yediyurappa became the Leader of the Opposition, helping his party to consolidate his Lingayat community's support.

The BJP first tasted power in Karnataka in 2006 when it brought down the Congress party government led by Dharam Singh in partnership with the Janata Dal (S) and formed a coalition government. He became the Deputy Chief Minister in the H.D. Kumaraswamy government. While he was supposed to become the Chief Minister in 2007, Kumaraswamy reneged on his promise, leading to the President's rule. Yediyurappa and Kumaraswamy buried their differences to come together in November 2007. But within a few days of Yediyurappa's oath as the Chief Minister, the J.D. (S) pulled the plug on the BJP government.

The sympathy for the BJP helped it to win 110 seats in the

2008 Assembly elections, precisely the number of seats where it lost deposits in the 1983 elections. Four years later, however, Yediyurappa was forced to leave the party due to the corruption allegations against him. He launched a new political party, Karnataka Janata Paksha, which contested the 2013 Karnataka Assembly elections, which proved disastrous for the BJP. His re-entry to the BJP swung the party back to power. Even at his ripe age of eight decades, Yediyurappa is so crucial for the BJP in Karnataka that he finds a place in the party's Parliamentary Committee, and his son B.Y. Vijayendra has been made the State unit chief to improve its prospects in Karnataka in the 2024 General Elections.

Two other factors aided the rise of Right-wing politics in Karnataka. The emergence of Islamist terror modules like Indian Mujahideen and the Students Islamic Movement of India (SIMI), among others in Coastal Karnataka, led to the rise of anti-Islamic viewpoints in the state. Terrorists like the Bhatkal brothers, Abdul Qureshi, and Sadiq Sheikh, among others, who were found to be involved in bombings in Uttar Pradesh (2007), Jaipur (2008), Ahmedabad (2008), and Delhi (2008), had their roots in Coastal Karnataka. The local Muslim connection with terrorism aggravated a feeling of anti-Muslim sentiment, driving the average Karnataka voter closer to the BJP. Though the BJP once forced its Chief Minister, Yediyurappa, to resign on the charges of corruption, the average voter was not dissuaded away from the saffron party due to the prevalence of anti-Muslim sentiment. In addition to this, the presence of people like Pramod Muthalik, who runs Sriram Sene, a Right-wing Hindutva group which resorts to moral policing, is keeping the anti-Muslim and anti-West mindset alive in Karnataka.

After Munugode, the Telangana unit of the BJP needed a win in Karnataka to spread the narrative that the party is a force to reckon with even in south India. The Karnataka Assembly elections were held on May 10, 2023, to elect all 224 Legislators. The BJP sidelined Yediyurappa as it hoped that the party could retain power based on the image of Prime Minister Narendra Modi. The party may have realised Yediyurappa's indispensability in the middle of the election campaign, which forced Modi to make last-ditch efforts to bring the Karnataka strongman into the campaign. But it was too late.

The Congress party, which now had a new party president, an astute Mallikarjun Kharge, ran a focused campaign across Karnataka. Kharge, a native of Karnataka and a person from the Scheduled Caste community who rose to the top from the bottom, worked for the Congress party. Kharge's speeches, Rahul Gandhi's outreach, and the well-coordinated and rightly orchestrated synergy between Siddaramaiah and D.K. Shivakumar aided the Congress party in securing a comfortable win. On the other hand, the BJP campaign revolved around Halal, Hijab, Tipu Sultan, and Islamic terror. Modi brought 'The Kerala Story' movie into the poll campaign to create an anti-Muslim sentiment among the people of Karnataka.

The election witnessed a total voter turnout of 73 per cent, which stood as the highest ever in the history of Karnataka and went in favour of the Congress party. In an Assembly of 224 seats, the Congress party won a comfortable 135 seats with close to 43 per cent votes, a net increase of 55 seats from the 2018 elections. The BJP, the single largest party that won slightly lower than the halfway mark in 2018, has now lost 38 seats to stand at a tally of 66. Interestingly, the BJP retained the percentage of votes in 2018 and 2023. Credit for this is solely attributed to the campaign blitzkrieg of Narendra Modi, who ran the entire campaign in his name. The party that suffered the most in this election was the Janata Dal (Secular) of former Prime Minister H.D. Deve Gowda and his family. Interestingly, the Janata Dal (Secular), portrayed as a marginal player, lost almost 50 per cent of its seats and fell to 19 seats, a net loss of 18 seats, compared to 2018 results. Political pundits, election observers, and media personnel noticed that the Muslims, especially those in the Old Mysore region and other regions where Deve Gowda has a significant clout, moved towards the Congress party. Being a marginal player and failing to attract Muslim votes had implications for the electoral outcome of the Telangana elections.

After the Karnataka debacle, the BJP changed its approach in Telangana. The party met with close shrugs from leaders of the BRS and the Congress party on joining the saffron brigade. Etela Rajender, who was responsible for wooing leaders from other parties, expressed his inability. Speaking to media persons, Etela Rajender said that instead of others joining the BJP, many prominent individuals invited him to move out of the saffron party to rejoin the BRS or join the Congress party.

With no possible headway, the BJP made a strategic blunder of changing the State unit president. The party replaced Bandi Sanjay, who brought great enthusiasm into the cadres across Telangana, with Union Minister G. Kishan Reddy, who failed to enthuse the party cadres during his earlier terms as the State unit chief. Many political observers and media personnel expressed disbelief over this move and immediately wrote the BJP off in this election. People who follow politics closely felt that the BJP decided to check their progress and let the BRS off the hook. A common argument on this issue was that the BJP did not want the benefits of the anti-incumbency mood they helped build to go to the Congress party, which was standing as the natural alternative to the BRS government.

With the Bharatiya Janata Party losing in Karnataka, its Telangana unit went into disarray, which cost the party a golden opportunity. Towards the end of the campaign, the saffron brigade paraded all prominent leaders, including Prime Minister Narendra Modi, Home Minister Amit Shah, Uttar Pradesh Chief Minister Yogi Adityanath, and Assam Chief Minister Himanta Biswa Sarma. They did what they were best at, giving rabble-rousing speeches to rake up Hindutva sentiment among the people. The Prime Minister addressed a few public meetings across the State and conducted a three-kilometre roadshow in Hyderabad on the penultimate day of the campaign.

For the Congress party, on the other hand, the election victory in Telangana has emerged as a litmus test that could validate its strategy of running the political campaign on time-bound poll promises. The Karnataka leaders played a crucial role in the election campaign in Telangana, with Chief Minister Siddaramaiah and Deputy Chief Minister D.K. Shivakumar actively put in their efforts. The Karnataka Congress party believed that the outcome in Telangana could be influenced by the success of their poll strategy of highlighting the party's policies in Karnataka.

Following their assumption of power, the Congress party government in Karnataka initiated the implementation of promised welfare schemes, including subsidised electricity, Rs 2,000 assistance to women heads of all families, free bus travel for women, and 10 kg of free rice. Taking a cue from this, the Telangana Congress party promised welfare initiatives ahead of the election, effectively countering the Bharat Rashtra Samithi's (BRS) array of schemes.

As part of the campaign, several leaders from Karnataka, including Dinesh Gundu Rao, Priyank Kharge, K.H. Muniyappa, Krishna Byre Gowda, Eshwara Khandre, M.C. Sudhakar, Sharan Prakash Patil, and B. Nagendra, actively participated in election campaigns on the ground in Telangana. The focus of Karnataka leaders was on showcasing the successful implementation of the five poll promises in their home state.

Despite the BRS's attacks alleging the party's failure to implement the poll promises, the Congress party confidently asserted that it had fulfilled its commitments, gaining the voters' trust. Members of the Karnataka Pradesh Congress Committee (KPCC) believed that the people of Karnataka have understood that the Congress party delivers on its promise. Though the BRS attacked the Congress party, claiming the programmes were a failure, Telangana results validate public opinion about the party in the states south of Vindhyas. The positive resonance of Congress party's successful implementation of welfare programs prevailed among voters in Telangana.

Turncoats and tickets

The 2023 Telangana State Assembly elections were remarkable in many aspects. One of them is the emergence of turncoats as a decisive factor in the victory of political parties. Quite a few among these turned to the Congress party, which obliged these individuals despite a certain degree of resistance from old-timers in their constituencies.

According to a few sources in the Congress party, the candidate's winnability was the lone criterion. If the main contender available in the party was unlikely to win the election, the party did not hesitate to bring in a "better alternative" to ensure the party won the seat. While no one in the Congress party officially admitted it, the party scrutinised the candidate's financial ability, prioritising his loyalty towards the party or the goodwill they carry locally in the constituency before allocating the ticket to contest.

While the ruling Bharat Rashtra Samithi, too, gave tickets to turncoats, these were incumbent legislators who won on a Congress party ticket and later joined the BRS, attributing their decision to the need to align with the ruling party for the development of the constituency. Two legislators who won a Telugu Desam Party ticket also joined the BRS. These defections into the BRS occurred within the first year of KCR's second term as the Chief Minister.

One of the most prominent political leaders who joined the

Congress party was Komatireddy Rajgopal Reddy. He returned to the Congress party to contest the Munugode Assembly seat, which was discussed in the chapter "Bypolls & Munugode". But his return upset local leaders, and they switched to other parties, hoping to find better opportunities.
Chalamalla Krishna Reddy, who was hoping to get the Congress party ticket, was the most affected by Rajgopal's homecoming. As he was denied a Congress party poll ticket, Krishna Reddy joined the BJP, which fielded him from Munugode. In his support, Union Home Minister Amit Shah participated in a roadshow and a public meeting organised at Choutuppal, the lone urban segment in the constituency.

Palvai Sravanthi, the Congress party candidate in the 2022 Munugode by-election, was also upset with Rajgopal's reentry. The BRS jumped in to invite a disgruntled Sravanthi into its fold. A day before she joined the BRS, Palvai Sravanthi said the present Congress party was not the same as the one to which her father, the late Palvai Goverdhan Reddy, gave his entire life. Her father won the Munugode seat five times for the party.

She further alleged that the Congress party has not adhered to its 'Jaipur Declaration', which categorically stated that no two members from the same family would be given tickets to contest. She also claimed that the party flouted its 'AICC Resolution', which promised a party ticket in the general election to the same candidate who would have fought a by-election in the most testing times for the party. The next day, BRS Working President Kalvakuntla Taraka Rama Rao personally welcomed her into the party along with her supporters.

Another prominent turncoat in these elections was Mynampally Hanumantha Rao, whose request to grant a Medak Assembly ticket to his son Mynampally Rohith Rao, along with his own from Malkajgiri seat, was turned down by the BRS. Though KCR announced Hanumanth Rao's candidature from the party in Malkajgiri, the latter expressed his displeasure over his son not being considered for the Medak seat. The Congress party, especially TPCC chief Revanth Reddy's team, quickly contacted the father-son duo and invited them to join the party.

Hanumantha Rao and his son joined the Congress party on September 28, 2023, and both were granted the tickets of their choice to contest. Several leaders, who had been working for a long time in the Congress party, were disappointed by this decision. Congress party's Malkajgiri unit president Nandikanti Sridhar and Medak unit chief Kantareddy Thirupathi Reddy resigned from the party and joined the Bharat Rashtra Samithi. These leaders, too, alleged that the Congress party had lost its past values and did not respect its resolutions.

The third prominent leader in this list is Gaddam Vivekanand, who is known as G. Vivek Venkatswamy. A former member of Lok Sabha from the Peddapalli Constituency on behalf of the Congress party is known to have moved across all three prominent political parties in Telangana.

Originally from the Congress party, Vivek shifted to the TRS once his party's prospects started dwindling. When the TRS denied him a ticket to contest from the Peddapalli Constituency in the 2019 Lok Sabha elections, a disappointed Vivek moved to the BJP, where he stayed put for over four years. While in the BJP, Vivek joined the chorus of turncoat leaders who vowed to dislodge KCR from power. They claimed that the BJP was the only alternative to the BRS in Telangana and that the Congress party had lost steam in the state.

Vivek was made a member of the National Executive Board of the BJP, a prominent position in the party. But, on realising that the BJP had lost its wind in the State and people did not see it as the party which could defeat KCR, Vivek switched back to the Congress party. Like Rajgopal Reddy, Vivek said his return to the Congress party is required to defeat KCR.

The most significant aspect of Vivek's joining the Congress party is that he made this move just a few days before the deadline for filing nominations to contest in the elections. Once Vivek was announced as the Congress party candidate, turmoil began in the Chennur Assembly Constituency in the Mancherial district. Many local leaders claimed that Vivek lost connection with the grassroots Congress party workers, and the prospects of him winning this seat will be tough.

Interestingly, on November 21, 2023, just a week before the polling, officials from the Enforcement Directorate, which falls under the Union government, carried out searches at the residence and offices of Vivek, along with the homes of his relatives and aides. Balka Suman, the BRS candidate, filed a complaint against Vivek, accusing him of using monetary inducements to win over the voters.

The most anticipated and highly-publicised entry into the Congress party was that of Ponguleti Srinivasa Reddy, the former member of Lok Sabha from Khammam Constituency. Srinivasa Reddy, who started his electoral politics with a win in the 2014 general elections from the Khammam Parliament seat on a YSR Congress party ticket, moved to the BRS along with two MLAs after its party chief Y.S. Jagan Mohan Reddy decided to put his Telangana ambitions in cold storage and to focus only on Andhra Pradesh.

However, KCR denied Srinivasa Reddy a ticket to contest from the Khammam Lok Sabha Constituency in 2019, leaving him disgruntled. After sulking for a while, Srinivasa Reddy made certain remarks against his party leadership. Though he did not criticise anyone personally, KCR suspended him from the party on April 9, 2023, along with another former minister, Jupally Krishna Rao.

On the invitation of PCC chief Revanth Reddy, Srinivasa Reddy joined the Congress party on July 3, 2023, in the presence of Rahul Gandhi, at a public meeting attended by thousands of his followers. Srinivasa Reddy and the Congress party turned the event into a show of strength. Along with Rahul Gandhi, AICC in-charge for Telangana affairs Manikrao Thakre, Revanth Reddy, members of Parliament from adjacent Nalgonda district N Uttam Kumar Reddy and Komatireddy Venkat Reddy, and balladeer Gaddar were present to welcome Srinivasa Reddy into the Congress party.

Interestingly, this meeting also marked the culmination of the 109-day-long 'padayatra' undertaken by the Congress Legislature Party leader Mallu Bhatti Vikramarka. Initially, the party was confused over fielding Srinivasa Reddy from Paleru or the two other general seats, Khammam and Kothagudem.

One of the reasons for the confusion was Y.S. Sharmila Reddy's interest in contesting from the Paleru Constituency. Sharmila Reddy is one of the well-known leaders in Telugu states as she is the daughter of former Chief Minister, the late Dr Y.S. Rajasekhara Reddy. Though she floated the YSR Telangana Party to begin her independent political career in Telangana, her well-wishers convinced her to merge her party with the Congress party to prevent the split in opposition votes.

As the Congress party planned to offer a more prominent role to Sharmila Reddy, the party put the announcement on Paleru on hold until it convinced her about it. After a long wait, the Congress party declared Srinivasa Reddy its candidate for the Paleru Assembly seat, where he was to face a stiff contest from incumbent MLA and BRS candidate Kandala Upender Reddy.

Jupally Krishna Reddy, who holds a unique record of winning from the Kollapur Assembly Constituency five times in a row, was another turncoat leader who rejoined the Congress party in the election year and got the ticket to contest from the seat of his choice. He served as a minister in the erstwhile united Andhra Pradesh and Telangana.

Krishna Rao won from the Kollapur Constituency in 1999, 2004, and 2009 general elections, 2012 by-polls, and again in 2014 general elections. However, he lost the seat in 2018. However, Krishna Rao, the Panchayat Raj and Rural Development minister in the KCR Cabinet between 2014 and 2018, was sidelined after losing to Congress party candidate Bhiram Harshvardhan Reddy in 2018. His position in the BRS became untenable after Harshvardhan Reddy, who defeated him, joined the BRS. He grew vocal in his criticism against Harshvardhan Reddy, who got the BRS ticket according to KCR's decision to offer poll tickets to all incumbent legislators with a few exceptions.

The BRS suspended him along with Ponguleti Srinivasa Reddy on the charges of indiscipline and dissent activities after he participated in a public meeting organised by the Khammam rebel. On August 3, 2023, Krishna Rao formally joined the Congress party in the presence of party president Mallikarjun Kharge, AICC General Secretary K.C. Venugopal, and Revanth Reddy. Speaking to the media after joining the Congress party, Krishna Rao alleged that the Chief Minister has ruined the state, and the people of Telangana have decided to vote out the BRS.

Thummala Nageswara Rao, who worked all his life against the Congress party, joined the party he fought just before the elections and walked away with the ticket to contest from the high-profile Khammam seat.

Nageswara Rao started his political career with the Telugu Desam Party during the N.T. Rama Rao era and won his first election to the State Assembly in 1985. He was a minister in the Cabinets of three different Chief Ministers. Nageswara Rao held high-profile portfolios like minor irrigation, heavy and medium irrigation, roads and buildings, and excise, among others, under N.T. Rama Rao, Nara Chandrababu Naidu, and K. Chandrashekhar Rao.

Nageswara Rao was wooed into the Telangana Rashtra Samithi in 2014 by KCR, his former colleague from the Telugu Desam era. KCR had expressed his desire to bring in individuals like Nageswara Rao, who had vast experience holding high-profile ministerial berths.

Apart from administrative experience, KCR felt that Nageswara Rao could strengthen the TRS in Khammam district, where the Telangana sentiment was weak due to its geographical proximity and cultural links to the Andhra region. Initially, Nageswara Rao was a member of the Legislative Council. However, he was allowed to fight from the Paleru Assembly segment in 2016 when the incumbent Congress party MLA Ramreddy Venkat Reddy died due to illness. In the by-election that followed, Nageswara Rao defeated the widow of Venkat Reddy and became MLA. However, in the 2018 elections, Nageswara Rao lost his Paleru seat to Congress party candidate Kandala Upender Reddy by 7,669 votes.

Like a few other Congress party legislators, Kandala Upender Reddy also defected to the BRS, much to the chagrin of Nageswara Rao. Though Nageswara Rao counted on the possibility of KCR, his friend of four decades, considering him for the Paleru or Khammam seats. But, once KCR decided to go with incumbents, Nageswara Rao quit his friend's party to join the Congress party that he fought against for four decades. Nageswara Rao joined the Congress party on September 16, 2023, in the presence of Congress party president Mallikarjun Kharge in Hyderabad and was given the Khammam ticket after great speculation.

K. Vijaya Reddy is one of the prominent women leaders who quit the Bharat Rashtra Samithi to join the Congress party for an election ticket. She is the daughter of former Congress Legislature Party chief and Hyderabad strongman P. Janardhan Reddy, popularly known as PJR. After the death of PJR, his son P Vishnuvardhan Reddy became an MLA from the Jubilee Hills Assembly segment. PJR's daughter Vijaya Reddy joined politics and shifted parties before joining the Congress party in 2023.

Vijaya Reddy started her political career as an independent candidate and joined the YSR Congress party in 2012. In 2014, Vijaya Reddy joined the TRS and became a corporator in the Greater Hyderabad Municipal Corporation. Her ambition to contest an Assembly seat motivated her to join the Congress party on June 23, 2022, after there were indications that KCR would repeat incumbent Danam Nagendra from the Khairatabad seat.

Similarly, there were candidates across all political parties who shifted parties in the election year or the year before with an eye on contesting from the Assembly seat of their choice.

Dr Kuchukulla Rajesh Reddy, son of a BRS MLC Kuchukulla Damodar Reddy, joined the Congress party in August 2023 and walked away with the ticket to contest from

Nagarkurnool seat, much to the discomfort of senior leader Nagam Janardhan Reddy.

When the Congress party announced Dr Rajesh Reddy's candidature, BRS Working President KTR and Finance Minister Harish Rao contacted Nagam Janardhan Reddy. They invited him back into the Bharat Rashtra Samithi. Janardhan Reddy, who was also an aspirant for the Congress party ticket from Nagarkurnool, stated that he felt deeply pained and humiliated for not being consulted before the party chose Dr Rajesh Reddy. Janardhan Reddy quit the Congress party and vowed to work for the BRS's victory.

In Gadwal, Sarita Thirupathaiah, the chairperson of the Zilla Parishad, joined the Congress party from the BRS in July 2023. She was fielded to contest from the Gadwal Constituency. This decision, however, invited fierce opposition from Kuruva Vijay Kumar, a general secretary in the Telangana Pradesh Congress Committee and an aspirant for the Gadwal ticket. He conveyed his displeasure to the chairman of the screening committee. An aspirant for the Congress party ticket in Gadwal, Patel Prabhakar Reddy, Jogulamba Gadwal District Congress Committee president, resigned from the party membership in protest.

Kasireddy Narayan Reddy is another leader who got the Congress party ticket to contest from the Kalwakurthy Constituency immediately after joining the party. Narayan Reddy was elected as a member of the Legislative Council under the local bodies category in January 2022. He had completed one year and eight months of his six-year tenure and still had four years and four months to complete his six-year term. But he expressed his desire to contest the Assembly polls to the BRS leadership. As the BRS renominated most incumbent MLAs, including the local G. Jaipal Yadav, Narayan Reddy joined the Congress party. Dr Challa Vamsi Chand Reddy, former MLA from Kalwakurthy, who wields significant clout with the party's high command, has made way for Narayan Reddy, and both agreed to work together to ensure the Congress party wins the election.

The Revanth Era

"If the Congress loses in Telangana, I will take complete responsibility, and will stand as guilty before madam Sonia Gandhi."

– Anumula Revanth Reddy

(before Telangana State Assembly Elections 2023)

Owning a house in Jubilee Hills is everyone's dream in Hyderabad, and being a part of the Jubilee Hills Cooperative Housing Society is a status symbol. Over the years, many individuals, among whom few were active politicians, have been a part of or have led this prestigious society. But there was only one individual who, on getting elected as the president of this housing society, believed and confided to a close friend that he would one day become the Chief Minister!

Anumula Revanth Reddy, Telangana's second and new CM, ousted his one-time guru, Kalvakuntla Chandrashekhar Rao. This story was narrated by Prof. K Nageshwar, a well-known political analyst with whom Revanth Reddy shared the bench in the erstwhile Andhra Pradesh State Legislative Council. Revanth Reddy had never been in a ruling party in his 17-year-long political career and had yet to hold an administrative post before this election. His rivals often consider his dreams outlandish. But he proved to the world that you can achieve big only if you dream big! Revanth Reddy, a leader with a chequered political past, changed the fortunes of the Congress party and ensured the grand old party of India won Telangana on the day when it suffered massive setbacks in the Hindi heartland. With the Congress party losing miserably in Rajasthan, Chhattisgarh, and Madhya Pradesh, the victory in Telangana emerged as the bright spot for the party. While the Congress party failed to retain power in Rajasthan and Chhattisgarh, the party could not defeat the Bharatiya Janata Party in Madhya Pradesh, where the BJP Chief Minister was expected to face a strong anti-incumbency.

Revanth Reddy was born to Narsimha Reddy and Ramchandramma on November 8, 1969, in Kondareddypalli village in the Kalwakurthy Assembly Constituency of erstwhile Mahboobnagar district. He was fourth among seven siblings, including a sister. None from his agricultural family was into politics.

Revanth Reddy went to school in Kalwakurthy and graduated from AV College in Hyderabad in fine arts in 1992. During his college days, he was associated with the ABVP, the student wing of the BJP. He married Geeta Reddy, a niece of former Union minister and senior Congress party leader S. Jaipal Reddy, and the daughter of Padma Reddy, a well-known face in politics and business circles, on May 7, 1992. According to a news report, one of his close friends and roommate, now a senior RSS leader, helped Revanth Reddy win the heart of the woman, who has since been his most robust support.

The 54-year-old Revanth Reddy started his political career in 2002 when he got in contact with KCR and joined the agitation for Telangana state. He worked closely with KCR and expected the Kalwakurthy Assembly ticket in 2004, where the TRS (now BRS) allied with the Congress party. At the last minute, the ticket was allocated to Yedam Kista Reddy, a close follower of Jaipal Reddy. It is widely believed that Jaipal Reddy was reluctant to cede Kalwakurthy's seat to the TRS and let Revanth Reddy contest from there in 2004. After that election, Revanth Reddy distanced himself from the TRS and decided to independently enter direct politics from the ground level. In 2006, he was elected to the Zilla Parishad Territorial Committee (ZPTC) from Midjil Mandal.

After about a year and a half, Revanth Reddy was elected as an independent member of the Legislative Council in the erstwhile united Andhra Pradesh under the local bodies' quota from Mahbubnagar as an independent and won. This was to be the turning point of his political career. He started his career when State politics was divided between the Congress party under the leadership of then chief minister Dr Y.S. Rajasekhara Reddy and the Telangana Desam Party under two-time chief minister Nara Chandrababu Naidu.

According to Prof. K Nageshwar, Revanth Reddy never came unprepared to the Legislative Council to participate in a discussion or talk on matters of public interest. This quality of Revanth Reddy and his sharp attack on the then government endeared him to Chandrababu Naidu. In 2007, the then chief minister, Dr Y S Rajasekhara Reddy, invited Revanth Reddy to the Congress party. However, the latter instead chose to join the opposition Telugu Desam. According to people close to him, Revanth Reddy wanted to express himself more and thought joining the opposition ranks would give him that opportunity.

Chandrababu Naidu fielded a young Revanth Reddy from Kodangal Constituency in Mahbubnagar district in the 2009 State Assembly elections, which the latter won, defeating five-time MLA Gurunath Reddy of the Congress party.

Interestingly, Revanth Reddy, in an interview he once gave to "Outlook", mentioned that when Chandrababu Naidu asked him to contest from Kodangal, he did not even know where that constituency was. Yet, he won the seat for the Telugu Desam Party, and there was no looking back for this leader.

Revanth Reddy was among the most preferred and watched spokespersons on regional television. His suave nature endeared him to the people who watched him speak. He was considered a brilliant politician with a bright future. In 2014, when Telangana was being formed, Revanth Reddy again won from Kodangal against Gurunath Reddy on a Telugu Desam Party ticket. With 15 MLAs in the State Assembly, Revanth Reddy was made the floor leader of the TDP in the Telangana State Assembly.

While the political alignment in the two Telugu states was settling down, and the people in both Telangana and Andhra Pradesh were adjusting to the new reality, which was welcomed by one region and opposed by the other, a major controversy broke, which would change the life and future of Revanth Reddy forever.

The Anti-Corruption Bureau of Telangana took Revanth Reddy into custody on May 31, 2015, claiming they had arrested him red-handed while offering to pay Rs 50 lakh in cash to Elvis Stephenson, an Anglo-Indian MLA in the Telangana State Assembly. It was alleged that Revanth Reddy made this offer to influence Stephenson to vote in favour of TDP candidate Vem Narender Reddy in the Telangana Legislative Council elections scheduled for June 1, 2015. A video of Revanth Reddy allegedly offering the cash was made public by the ACB officials, along with an audio conversation between Stephenson and TDP supremo and the then chief minister of Andhra Pradesh Chandrababu Naidu.

This was undoubtedly the darkest phase in Revanth Reddy's life. His arrest took place just before the marriage of his daughter. The visuals of Revanth Reddy's arrest, his reaction, his statements, and his challenge to KCR were revisited by many on the day the Congress party, under the leadership of Revanth Reddy, defeated KCR. I, too, wrote this chapter on the same day – that is December 2, 2023.

With a major shift in his political prospects and the political outfit he then represented, Revanth Reddy quit the Telugu Desam Party and joined the Congress party in October 2017. In 2018, the Congress party fielded him from the Kodangal Constituency. However, the ruling Telangana Rashtra Samithi and KCR applied every possible tactic to ensure Revanth Reddy lost to the TRS' Patnam Narender Reddy.

Though losing his seat was seen as another setback for Revanth Reddy, this defeat improved his political career. The Congress party fielded Revanth Reddy from the Malkajgiri Lok Sabha Constituency in the 2019 general elections, a seat he won comfortably. This win took Revanth Reddy to Parliament, bringing him closer to Rahul Gandhi first and then to Sonia Gandhi and Priyanka Gandhi. Since his arrest in 2015, Revanth Reddy has changed. He was brash and, at times, abusive when it came to talking about KCR or his family members, especially KTR, Harish Rao, and Santhosh Rao.

In 2021, with no headway in sight, the Congress party changed the guard in Telangana State. The party replaced Nalamada Uttam Kumar Reddy, one of the longest-serving presidents of the Telangana Pradesh Congress Committee, with Revanth Reddy. Those were times when many senior Congress party leaders like Komatireddy Venkat Reddy, D.K. Aruna, and others were eyeing the post. Everyone in the Congress party was surprised over the party high command's choice, which since 2023 has been hailed as the masterstroke.

Since becoming TPCC chief, Revanth Reddy had his task cut out, and now it is evident that he was clear about his target, which was to dethrone KCR from the post of Chief Minister of Telangana. In 2022, though there was a change of guard with Mallikarjun Kharge, a party veteran, coming in as the president of the Congress party in place of Sonia Gandhi, nothing changed for Revanth Reddy.

In the run-up to the 2023 Telangana State Assembly elections, Revanth Reddy faced numerous challenges from within the party. During an unexpected yet long interaction I had with Revanth Reddy in March 2023, he stated, "Raghav, my problem is not KCR or BJP; my main problem is the leaders within the Congress party!"

In the election year, Revanth Reddy sidelined a few leaders he considered troublemakers or useless, made peace with those fighting who would drain his energies, and brought quite a few leaders from the BRS and the BJP into the Congress party fold. Revanth Reddy, in this process, displayed his absolute control over the Congress party, and the party's high command, too, did not disturb him at any stage. Revanth Reddy continued his game plan to dethrone KCR in Hyderabad while his political opponents wasted time in New Delhi. Revanth Reddy received complete support from Manick Rao Thakre, the party in charge of Telangana, and Sunil Kanugolu, the political strategist who shares credit for the brilliant campaign in the state.

Since he joined the Congress party, or ever since becoming the TPCC chief, Revanth Reddy has polarised opinions of his party colleagues in particular and Telangana in general. His proximity with Chandrababu Naidu in the past continued to haunt his image till the day of polling on November 30, 2023. Revanth Reddy was repeatedly asked about his closeness with the former AP chief minister during his numerous interviews.

Few people of the Reddy community in Telangana could not accept Revanth Reddy as their representative, and few even preferred to call him "Revanth Chowdary". The TPCC chief handled all these issues well, and during the numerous interviews, Revanth Reddy positioned himself as a colleague of Chandrababu Naidu, not an aide or a subordinate. Closer to the elections, it is widely believed that a large section of the Reddy community in Telangana stood behind Revanth Reddy and ensured a win for the Congress party. With the backing he received from within the party and noticing the mood of the people of Telangana, who were either vexed with the incumbent BRS government or fatigued with it, Revanth Reddy upped the ante. The TPCC chief possibly understood he had to humanise KCR and position him as a fallible personality. Using the people's mood, Revanth Reddy ridiculed the then chief minister by attributing all kinds of names. Revanth Reddy had to bring down the image of KCR and break the halo around his name, which BRS leaders and cadres built over a decade.

While BRS wanted KCR to be positioned as "Telangana Jathi Pitha" or as "Bapu", Revanth Reddy tried to raze it down to the ground by calling him names like Thuglak, Bewakoof, Sannasi, Dadamma, among others. He even called members of the KCR family "economic terrorists", alleging corruption.

Revanth Reddy refused comparisons with Rama Rao during an interview with a national television channel. He claimed he reached his stage based on merit, while KTR is where he is because of his father's legacy. It was this spirit that endeared him to the youth of Telangana.

Before this, Revanth Reddy had run-ins with KTR on various issues. At an earlier instance, Rama Rao alleged that Revanth Reddy was only the face; the real person who was running the Congress party in Telangana was K.V.P. Ramachandra Rao, a former Rajya Sabha member and someone who was once considered the alter-ego of the late Dr Y S Rajasekhara Reddy. Revanth Reddy was quick to counter this allegation and, in turn, stated that it was KTR and KCR who were trying to mislead the people of Telangana. Revanth Reddy even alleged that the KCR government, on the recommendations of KVP, had appointed some officers in certain departments. He also hit out at the KCR government, stating that the party has mortgaged the interests of Telangana to leaders and contractors from the Andhra region.

Revanth Reddy was quick and effective in countering any allegation against him or the Congress party. He used media efficiently to communicate with the people of Telangana. During an interview, Prof. K Nageshwar asked Revanth Reddy why he was not attacking the Bharatiya Janata Party. In his reply, Revanth Reddy said he needed to fight the KCR regime, bring him down, and not waste his energy by fighting the BJP, which was not a factor in the 2023 Telangana State Assembly polls. This clarity of thought helped Revanth Reddy stay focused.

In another interview with a regional channel, Revanth Reddy beautifully articulated the necessity of political leaders having compassion towards the people, which he alleged was lacking among the members of the KCR family. After the Telangana Public Service Commission paper leakage, which rocked the State and brought great disrepute to the KCR government, the TPCC chief was seen calling upon the youth and the unemployed in the State to join the Congress party to block the highway on October 16, 2023, in protest. Such instances and radical calls made by Revanth Reddy catapulted his and the Congress party's prospects in the State Assembly Elections.

Since he was appointed Telangana Pradesh Congress Committee (TPCC) chief in July 2021, Revanth Reddy has been the party's most visible face. He took out a Padayatra in the State and led street protests from the front. Taking a cue from the lesson it learned in Karnataka, where the visibility and prominence of the local Congress party leaders helped win the State Assembly elections, the party stuck to the game plan.

Despite voices of dissent against Revanth Reddy, the Congress party projected him as the leader for the big stage. He was made to address massive rallies across the state, and both Rahul Gandhi, Priyanka Gandhi, and Mallikarjun Kharge moved closer to Revanth Reddy. The TPCC always maintained that Telangana would witness a contest between only two parties in the State Assembly elections, and the BJP would not be a major contender. During the campaign, he went on assuring his party cadres that the Congress party would win 80+ seats, and his strategic approach in keeping the spirits of the cadres up paid off in the end.

Another central question Revanth Reddy faced during the campaign was how the Congress party if voted to power, would fulfil the six guarantees it made to the people of Telangana. The government must spend Rs 80,000 crore to implement its six guarantees. However, Revanth Reddy was confident about meeting the cost and stated that there are many "central schemes" that the KCR government did not utilise. Revanth Reddy claimed that grants and matching grants or loans, including those for irrigation, health, education, SC/ST welfare, and several other schemes, are readily available.

Telangana is a drought-prone state, and such states get grants up to 90 per cent for irrigation projects under the Accelerated Irrigation Benefits Programme (AIBP), which was first launched in the year 1996-97 to provide central assistance to states for the major/medium irrigation projects in the Country. The core objective is accelerating the implementation of advanced-stage irrigation projects that are held up due to financial constraints.

The Pradhan Mantri Krishi Sinchayee Yojana (PMKSY) was launched in 2015-16, and the Accelerated Irrigation Benefits Programme (AIBP) was coopted in it. Revanth Reddy alleged that KCR never sent any proposal to the Union government, which is duty-bound to release funds towards input subsidies to farmers and compensation for crop losses, among others.

Having backed Revanth Reddy, a powerful orator with solid community support, it is learnt that the Congress party, through its President Mallikarjun Kharge and Organisational Secretary K.C. Venugopal, told Congress party leaders in Telangana to paper over the differences and show a united face. At the same time, Revanth Reddy was also told to shed his "autocratic" ways and penchant to promote his supporters. The closing of ranks by the warring State leaders coincided with internal surveys of the party after the Karnataka verdict, showing the build-up of an anti-incumbency mood in Telangana. The run-up to the elections saw little infighting, a rarity in the Congress party.

Revanth Reddy and the Congress Legislative Party leader Mallu Bhatti Vikramarka took out separate yantras. However, there was little public acrimony, though most senior State leaders remained antagonistic to Revanth Reddy, who joined the Congress party only in 2017. Unlike in Rajasthan and Madhya Pradesh, there was very little jostling among leaders, even during the ticket distribution. This is mainly because the party did not have powerful satraps who could stare the high command in the eye. Also, the central leadership kept a close eye on the State at every campaign stage.

Even hardcore critics of Revanth Reddy admit he is a charismatic and powerful orator. A leader with stints in the Telugu Desam Party and the Telangana Rashtra Samithi, he was handed over the reins of the party in 2021, just four years after crossing sides. His sharpest critics admit that many factors came together in Revanth Reddy's favour.

The TPCC chief's critics suggest that the Congress party's graph changed dramatically after the Karnataka elections. It is not about one individual playing, but ultimately, the enthusiasm of the party cadres and the leadership helped the man sitting at the top. Though Revanth Reddy had been at the helm since 2021, it was only after the Congress party's victory in the Karnataka elections that the graph began to change, and his fortune changed for good. A good orator with a deep understanding of issues in Telangana and an ability to connect with the masses, popularity among the youth endeared Revanth Reddy to the cadres of the Congress party. It allowed him to emerge as one of few Congress party leaders with a bright future.

The Campaign

The importance of election campaigns built around catchy slogans and simple promises in India, where literacy is still lower than in sub-Saharan countries like Zimbabwe, cannot be understated. Several catchy slogans like Indira Gandhi's *"Woh kehte hain 'Indira hatao'; main kehti hoon' Garibi Hatao"*, Atal Behari Vajpayee-led BJP's focus on being a party with a difference, Sonia Gandhi-led Congress party's *'Aam Aadmi Ko Kya Mila'* have successfully made history.

Similarly, the Congress party's campaign in the Telangana State Assembly Elections will stand among the best political campaigns in 21st-century India. Its election campaign song *"Maarpu Kavali, Congress Ravali"* (We want change, Congress must come) became a sensation across Telangana. This catchy number became so popular that even schoolchildren in villages in Telangana were seen to be humming it.

Another campaign that proved to be effective was an advertisement of the Congress party, which highlighted the plight of marginal farmers due to the 'Dharani Portal' started by the KCR government. The Congress party's commercial video showcased the agrarian crisis in Telangana, the 8,000 farmer suicides, and issues like fertiliser purchase and paddy procurement. It ended with the party's promise of a loan waiver to benefit all marginal farmers. Similarly, the Congress party campaign has effectively communicated its Six Guarantees to Telangana voters and drilled in their minds how they will bring a quality difference to their lives.

While the Congress party formally released its election manifesto less than two weeks before the elections, the party began its campaign months ahead by getting its top leaders, like Rahul Gandhi and Priyanka Gandhi, to launch various declarations aimed at specific groups such as farmers, unemployed youth, women among others. The Declarations detailed how it intends to solve people's problems.
The Congress party formally released its manifesto on November 17, 2023, less than two weeks before the State goes to polls. The Congress party's Six Guarantees promised were categorised as follows:

1. Mahalakshmi scheme aims at the women of Telangana. Under this scheme, the Congress party promised to give Rs 2,500 to every eligible woman. Deliver gas cylinders to every household for just Rs 500. It offered free travel for women in RTC buses. The Aam Aadmi Party government first introduced the free bus travel scheme in New Delhi, followed by the Congress party government in Karnataka.

2. Rythu Bharosa aims at the farmers of Telangana. Under this scheme, the Congress party promised to give Rs 15,000 per acre to land-holding farmers and tenant farmers in the state. It also promised Rs 12,000 per year to agriculture labour. It also promised a bonus of Rs 500 per year on paddy production. In addition, during an election campaign meeting in Warangal, Rahul Gandhi announced that the Congress party would provide free electricity to the farmers when it came into power in Telangana. One of the major contributors to KCR's return to power in 2018 was his 'Rythu Bandhu' scheme. This initiative, later adopted by

Prime Minister Narendra Modi, was a game changer for the farmers. Many small and medium farmers commend the initiative, which provides much-needed financial input into farming.

3. Gurha Jyothi aims at the women in Telangana. Under this scheme, the Congress party promised to provide 200 units of free electricity to every household in the state.

4. Indiramma Indlu aims at people with low incomes in Telangana. Under this scheme, the Congress party promised 250 square yards of land to all those who laid down their lives during the agitations for a separate Telangana State. The party also assured of a house site and Rs 5 lakh to people without a house.

5. Yuva Vikasam targets the youth of Telangana. Under this scheme, the Congress party promised to launch a Vidya Bharosa card worth Rs 5 lakh for students pursuing higher education. Setting up Telangana International Schools in every Mandal across the State is another feature of the Yuva Vikasam promise.

6. Cheyutha aims at older people in Telangana. Under this scheme, the Congress party promised a Rs 4,000 monthly pension to the senior citizens and offered Rs 10 lakh health insurance under the Rajiv Aarogyasri initiative.

Commenting on the Six Guarantees, which proved to be the game changer for the party, Mallikarjun Kharge said the Congress party is determined to provide social justice, economic empowerment, and unbridled progress to the people of Telangana. He also claimed that the Congress party created Telangana, and it will not let the struggle and sacrifice of the movement go in vain due to the Commission Raj and the loot of the BRS. Kharge even stated that the Congress party's Six Guarantees will help realise the dream of Bangaru Telangana.

Unemployment was and is a major issue in Telangana. The main catalyst for separate Telangana state demand was unemployment. During the campaign, the Congress party promised to fill two lakh vacancies in the State government within the first year of its rule.

The party assured the youth of Telangana that the infamous State Public Service Commission, which became the centre of several controversies, would be revamped along the lines of the Union Public Service Commission.

Congress party leaders, in general, and Revanth Reddy, in particular, stated that its government would fill all vacancies in the government transparently within the stipulated time frame without giving scope for any controversies.

What proved to be a clincher idea was that the Congress party, to reiterate its commitment to resolving the unemployment issue in the state, released a mock 'job calendar'. Congress party president Mallikarjun Kharge, along with Revanth Reddy, were present on the occasion to release the 'Congress Job Calendar' to lend more credibility to their promise. The calendar released as a part of their election manifesto titled 'Abhaya Hastam', looked as below:

Congress 'Job Calendar'	
Recruitment	Notification date
Group-I	February 1, 2024
Group-II Phase 1	April 1, 2024
Group-II Phase 2	December 15, 2024
Group-III Phase 1	June 1, 2024
Group-III Phase 2	December 15, 2024
Group-IV Phase 1	June 1, 2024
Group-IV Phase 2	December 1, 2024
Other vacancies to be filled between May 1, 2024 and December 25, 2024	

The Congress party has highlighted the unemployment issue all through its campaign. Though the transformation of the Congress party in Telangana began with Bharat Jodo Yatra, which passed through the State in the last quarter of 2022, the party reaped its benefits in the second half of 2023.

Priyanka Gandhi announced a Youth Declaration in Hyderabad on May 8, 2023, pledging to address youth unemployment and set off its campaign to win Telangana. In the public meeting held at Saroornagar in Hyderabad, Priyanka Gandhi assured that if the Congress party fails to fulfil the promises, it will not come before the people of Telangana to seek power again. She said that the Congress party government would fight for the sacrifices of the martyrs and fulfil their dreams.

Hyderabad Youth Declaration: Key Points

- A government job for a family member of every Telangana martyr and a monthly stipend of Rs. 25,000 to the family
- Withdrawal of all cases against Telangana movement activists and issuance of identity cards to them
- Monthly allowance of Rs. 4,000 for unemployed youth
- Establishment of Telangana Public Service Commission with complete transparency
- Introduction of a central-level online registration system for unemployed youth
- Establishment of employment centres and skill training centres in every zone of the state
- Local candidates will get 75 per cent reservations in private institutions, and a youth commission will be formed to address the issues of youth.
- Interest-free loan of Rs. 10 lakh to be provided to the youth
- Special law to be enacted in Gulf countries for the rehabilitation of jobless people and action against fake agents
- Government guidance to be provided for employment in foreign countries
- Release of Rs. 4,000 crore for fee reimbursement dues of SC, ST, BC, and minority students
- Establishment of universities in Adilabad, Khammam, and Medak, and IIIT institutes at four places in TS
- Establishment of a sports university and universities for employees of Home Guard, RTC, and other institutions in Warangal and Hyderabad.

In her 35-minute-long speech, Priyanka Gandhi repeatedly remembered the sacrifices of the martyrs of Telangana and vowed to fulfil their dreams. She said Telangana is not just the name of a land, but the people give this land the status of mother. Hundreds of young people sacrificed their lives for their mother Telangana. In the name of employment, the Telangana movement was launched so that every section of society gets its rights and Dr. Ambedkar's vision of social justice is implemented. She said that every section of society participated in the Telangana struggle, and the State was formed due to their sacrifices. She also acknowledged that her family has made sacrifices for the country and understands the feelings of the sacrificial family.
Exactly a year before Priyanka Gandhi announced the Youth Declaration, in May 2022, Rahul Gandhi released the 'Warangal Declaration', which became the guiding light for the Congress party.

In various interviews Revanth Reddy gave to the media in the run-up to the elections, the TPCC chief stated that the party is committed to what it promised as part of the declaration it made in Warangal at the "Raithu Sangharshana Sabha". The major promise in that meeting was to waive off Rs 2 lakhs of each farmer's loans and buy paddy at the minimum support price. At this meeting, the Congress party first spoke about initiating a direct benefit of Rs 15,000 per acre of farmland to the farmers in Telangana.

While Revanth Reddy upped the momentum and sustained it for the Congress party over time, Rahul Gandhi complimented it with his digital and physical presence in Telangana. When a 23-year-old girl, a job aspirant, committed suicide in Hyderabad, Rahul Gandhi reacted quickly. He slammed the KCR-led BRS government, saying this was not a suicide but a murder of the dreams and aspirations of the youth.

Portraying himself as a commoner, Rahul Gandhi, during his campaign in Telangana, visited Bawarchi restaurant, a popular biryani place in Hyderabad, where he interacted with common people who visited the place. The same evening, Rahul Gandhi also visited the City Central Library to meet unemployed youth preparing for recruitment into government jobs. They shared their plight with the scion of the Nehru-Gandhi family. They highlighted the pain caused to them and their families due to the leakage of question papers from the Telangana State Public Service Commission.

Sharing details of his interaction with the youth, Rahul Gandhi posted on his official “X” handle: "Today in Ashoknagar, Hyderabad, I met the youth who are preparing for various competitive exams. I was moved by the fact that they had hoped that they would get success if Telangana came, but even 10 years after the state's arrival, their aspirations have not been fulfilled. The youth of Telangana have been among the worst affected by the misrule of the government over the past 10 years. But they are resilient and full of potential, as was evident from my interaction with them. It is our duty to transform their dreams into reality, which is why we have released a job calendar to fill 2 lakh government jobs within the first year of our government in Telangana. This is not just a promise; it is Congress party's guarantee!"

Unlike the Bharatiya Janata Party, the Congress party is considered a natural party in Telangana, with deep roots across the State for several decades. Though people did not give enough credit to the Congress party for creating the Telangana state in 2014, they now feel that the KCR-led Telangana Rashtra Samithi has taken disproportionate credit and acquired power two times.

Leaving no stone unturned and firing on all cylinders, Rahul Gandhi played his role smartly by convincing people that the BRS and AIMIM are the secret allies of the BJP. He called BRS as the 'BJP Rishtedar Samiti'. He accused the All India Majlis-e-Ittehadul Muslimeen (AIMIM) and its leader, Asaduddin Owaisi, an ally of the BRS, of being a hand-in-glove of the BJP.

The AIMIM, a Hyderabad-based political party, has been fielding dozens of its candidates across the country, where it finds Muslims to form a significant chunk of votes. In Telangana, where Muslims constitute 13 per cent of its population, having numerous constituencies with substantial numbers of Muslim voters, the AIMIM contested only nine seats.

To highlight the AIMIM's alleged game plan, Rahul Gandhi coined a new slogan, *"Modi ji ke hai do yaar, Owaisi aur KCR* (Modi has two friends: Owaisi and KCR)." This slogan gained traction among the Muslims of Telangana, who bought the Congress party's allegation. As KCR was engaging only with the AIMIM on issues of Muslims, other Muslim bodies like the Jamaat-e-Islami and the Tablighi Jamat supported a large number of Congress party candidates in the state.

Though the ruling Bharat Rashtra Samithi was the primary target of the Congress party in Telangana, Rahul Gandhi took a few blows at the BJP and its most famous face, Prime Minister Narendra Modi. In one such instance, Rahul Gandhi said it is a fight of ideology, and neither Modi nor he would compromise. Rahul Gandhi stated that he fights the hatred in the heart of Narendra Modi. There are 24 cases against him for fighting this hatred, including those in Assam, Gujarat, Bihar, and Maharashtra. He also brought to the people's notice that, for the first time, he was sentenced to two years of prison for defamation, which led to the cancellation of his Lok Sabha membership.

Another critical element that helped the Congress party is the state leadership. Or rather, a lack of strong leadership that arrogates a know-all attitude to itself. In Madhya Pradesh and Rajasthan, the Congress party had influential leaders like Kamal Nath and Ashok Gehlot, who ran the party campaign independently. In Telangana, however, the Congress party's central leadership was fully invested. They have been involved in election planning for over a year. It designed and executed a campaign modelled around 'five-tier surveillance' in Telangana, which helped the party to register a victory over the ruling Bharat Rashtra Samithi.

The party's central leaders, such as Congress President Mallikarjun Kharge, Rahul Gandhi, and Priyanka Gandhi, attended more campaign events in Telangana than in other states.

Rahul Gandhi attended at least 24 programmes spread over 10 days in Telangana, while he did 11 each for Rajasthan (in

4 days) and Madhya Pradesh (5 days). Priyanka attended 14 programmes in seven days as opposed to 12 in Madhya Pradesh (7 days), five in Chhattisgarh (3 days), and seven in Rajasthan (4 days). Kharge attended 11 in Telangana (6 days), eight in Rajasthan (5 days) and six each in Chhattisgarh and Madhya Pradesh (3 days each).

According to numerous reports from the ground, the Congress party had also excelled in the outreach programme, with its leaders, contestants, and workers visiting more voters' homes than the BRS and the BJP cadres. It is also observed that the Congress party's approach of blending their online campaign with their on-ground strategies played a decisive role in convincing the voters. Congress party general secretary (Organisation) K.C. Venugopal camped in Telangana to coordinate the efforts as key State leaders like Revanth Reddy and Bhatti Vikramarka were busy contesting the elections. He conducted daily review meetings with candidates and observers.

According to Congress party leaders, the Bharat Jodo Yatra and the subsequent Karnataka Assembly victory were game-changing moments for Telangana. Sources said senior leaders like Mallikarjun Kharge, Rahul Gandhi, Venugopal, Revanth Reddy and Bhatti Vikramarka first met to discuss a strategy a year ago. The meeting was followed up by statewide 'padayatras' under the leadership of Revanth Reddy and Bhatti Vikramarka and the appointment of State observers who conducted surveys to study people's sentiments on the BRS government.

A separate survey was conducted to identify prospective candidates for the elections. The central leadership has monitored the party activities at five levels. State observers looked at the big picture. While special observers were tasked to monitor activity at the Lok Sabha Constituency level, observers at every Assembly seat and observers for Assembly clusters kept a tight vigil at the micro level.

The party had appointed special observers to look into issues of minorities and marginalised in seats where they have substantial numbers. The leadership also analysed the winnability quotient in every seat, an exercise, leaders said, led to the identification of winning candidates. Venugopal also met around 15 rebel leaders, who were persuaded to support Congress party candidates by promising them that the party would take care of their interests.

With the experiences and learnings from the Karnataka State Assembly Elections, the Congress party established specific teams to talk to rebel candidates to convince them to withdraw in favour of the party candidates. The dissidents were offered other posts once the party came into power or an opportunity to contest in the Lok Sabha elections. The party managed to convince nine rebels to withdraw from the electoral race on the last day for the withdrawal of nominations. The rebels, who had filed nominations after failing to obtain tickets from the party to contest the Assembly elections, have withdrawn in favour of official candidates.

Adilabad, however, was the only exception where rebel Congress party candidate Sanjeev Reddy refused to withdraw from the electoral fray. There was high drama at the residence of Patel Ramesh Reddy, who had filed nomination from Suryapet when AICC national secretary Rohit Chaudhary and senior Congress party leader Mallu Ravi visited him. The leaders went to request him to withdraw from the race and support the party's official candidate, Ramreddy Damodar Reddy. But the supporters of Patel Ramesh Reddy grew violent and attacked 73-year-old Mallu Ravi after his request for a tete-e-tete. In the house, Patel Ramesh Reddy, his wife and others were crying and pleading with the leaders to support his candidature. After great persuasion, Ramesh Reddy finally withdrew from the race and agreed to accept the offer to contest in the Parliament elections to be held in April-May 2024.

Poll strategist Sunil Kanugolu was another factor in the Congress party's victory. He has proven to be the man with the Midas touch, plotting the Congress party's impressive turnaround in Telangana, just months after being the architect of the grand old party's return to power in Karnataka. Kanugolu was primarily credited for shaping the Congress party's win in Karnataka and was later accorded Cabinet rank in the Siddaramaiah government.

In Telangana, Kanugolu, along with the TPCC chief Revanth Reddy, formed a formidable pair to chalk out the Congress party's strategy to pull down the Kalvakuntla Chandrashekhar Rao-led BRS government that was eying a third term in the southern state. If the BRS had won, KCR would have been the first Chief Minister to be elected thrice in an Indian State south of Vindhyas.

Kanugolu had also made forays in Rajasthan and Madhya Pradesh following a directive from the party's central leadership. However, regional satraps Ashok Gehlot and Kamal Nath disagreed with the poll strategist's assessment and suggestions. In Rajasthan, Gehlot roped in Naresh Arora's Designbox to construct the Congress party government's narrative in his state.

Kanugolu's success in Karnataka and Telangana resulted from the free hand given to him and allowing his team to work freely. Kanugolu, who hails from Karnataka and is in his early 40s, has been mainly considered the brain behind the Congress party's narrative in Karnataka with the 'PayCM' campaign against the BJP. In the run-up to the polls in Telangana, he highlighted the alleged corruption of the KCR dispensation as part of Congress party's campaign that struck a chord with the people.

The Congress party campaigns in both Karnataka and Telangana have been very similar. Both highlighted the alleged corruption of the ruling dispensation and projected welfare guarantees that seemed to have struck an instant connection with the public. Kanugolu was also involved in several BJP poll campaigns in the past. In 2018, he worked with the BJP in Karnataka, and the party became the single-largest party with 104 seats. He also worked on Narendra Modi's campaign in 2014 and the party's political campaigns in Uttar Pradesh and Gujarat.

Kanugolu, a former consultant with McKinsey, was also associated with DMK chief MK Stalin and oversaw the party's 'Namakku Naame' (we are for ourselves) campaign during the 2019 Lok Sabha elections. In 2021, he also worked with the AIADMK against the DMK and led the party to win 75 seats in the Tamil Nadu Assembly elections.

Kanugolu joined the Congress party last year and worked closely with the Karnataka campaign. He is also credited with strategising Rahul Gandhi's cross-country 'Bharat Jodo Yatra' from Kanyakumari to Kashmir last year. Having delivered Karnataka and Telangana to the Congress party, Kanugolu is likely to be given more responsibilities by the party in the run-up to the Lok Sabha polls in April-May 2024.

KCR & KTR

Kalvakuntla Chandrashekhar Rao, known as KCR, is one of India's most charismatic and influential regional leaders. He was pivotal in forming and developing India's youngest state, Telangana. His journey from a grassroots politician to the Chief Minister of the State is a testament to his political acumen and commitment to the welfare of the people.

KCR began his political career in the early 1980s, actively participating in the Telugu Desam Party (TDP). However, disillusioned with the political dynamics, he eventually founded the Telangana Rashtra Samithi (TRS) in 2001. His primary goal was to advocate statehood for Telangana, citing regional disparities and neglect as the driving factors. He played a crucial role in the Telangana movement, a protracted struggle that sought to carve out a separate State from the composite Telugu State of Andhra Pradesh.

His leadership and relentless efforts mobilised the masses, creating a groundswell of support for the cause. The movement gained momentum, leading to Telangana achieving its long-overdue statehood on June 2, 2014.

KCR's unwavering commitment to the people of Telangana earned him the position of the first Chief Minister of the newly formed state. As the head of the government, he embarked on a mission to address the socio-economic challenges faced by the region. KCR's administration focused on irrigation projects, welfare schemes, and infrastructure development to uplift the standard of living for the people. Under KCR's leadership, Telangana witnessed the implementation of several flagship programmes and initiatives.

The "Mission Bhagiratha" project is aimed to provide safe drinking water to every household in the state, showcasing his dedication to improving the quality of life for the people.
Schemes like "Rythu Bandhu" and "KCR Kit" were introduced to support farmers and pregnant women, respectively. Focusing on economic development and industrial growth has also marked KCR's tenure.

Initiatives like the "TS-iPASS" (Telangana State Industrial Project Approval and Self-Certification System) were implemented to streamline the industrial clearance process, attracting investments and promoting job creation in the state.

A blend of vision, determination, and a deep-rooted commitment to the welfare of the people has characterised KCR's leadership in Telangana. His journey from a grassroots political activist to the Telangana Chief Minister reflects the transformative power of dedicated leadership. While KCR continues to face challenges and criticisms, his impact on the development and identity of Telangana remains a significant chapter in the political history of India.

In the last quarter of 2022, when the BRS was still known as the TRS, my friends and I, under the banner of our company, NITI Pollsters, surveyed 45 Assembly segments selected from across the state. The survey was conducted to assess the mood of people in Telangana one year before the State went to polls.

Many interesting aspects emerged from this survey, but the main takeaway was the growing dissatisfaction among the people with incumbent MLAs. One of the questions asked in the survey was whether the person participating would elect the incumbent MLA in 2023.

Interestingly, in some constituencies, close to 50 per cent of survey participants stated they had no qualms with the TRS or Chief Minister KCR but were distressed with the local MLAs for various reasons. These respondents informed the survey agents that they would wish the TRS to change the MLA candidate from these segments. If the TRS fields the same candidate in the 2023 Assembly elections, they will vote against them.

Our survey indicated that 42 per cent of voters are satisfied with the performance of the present MLAs. In comparison, 33 per cent have shown dissatisfaction, and 22 per cent of voters are neither satisfied nor dissatisfied with the performance of their present MLAs. The data collated in the survey revealed high anti-incumbency against the sitting MLAs in some Assembly segments. The finding showed that 47 per cent of the voters intended to re-elect their MLA, while 41 per cent wanted to change their MLA candidate. The gap was low, and the ruling TRS was required to do something about it. Compared to the male voters, more female voters wanted to change their MLAs. More young voters in the age group of 18 to 30 years wanted to change their MLAs. Except for the Scheduled Tribe Hindu voters, most of the voters of other social groups wanted to change their MLAs. By the time of the elections, the results showed that ST Hindus, too, rejected BRS. While most educated and urban or urbanised voters want to change their MLAs, most rural voters want to re-elect their MLA.

My friend, Nitin Tanksale, who leads the team at NITI Pollsters, brought our findings to KCR's notice during a long meeting with him in the second quarter of 2023.

Rated among the best political strategists in the country, Nitin Tanksale informed the Chief Minister that he must consider changing the MLA candidates to beat anti-incumbency in the state. Nitin, who spent more than 12 hours with KCR over two days discussing various aspects of State and national politics, tried to convince KCR that people were still willing to vote for the BRS government.

However, MLAs on the ground no longer enjoy the popular support. Despite this health warning, KCR, known to run administration and party in his style and with an iron fist, refused to accept any threat to his government. Numerous news reports in the two weeks before the polling and a week after the counting highlighted that K.T. Rama Rao requested his father to consider changing the MLA candidates in at least 30 to 35 Assembly segments to avoid any risk. It is learnt that KCR ignored the requests made by his heir apparent, too.

While KCR's decision had left many political analysts wondering, the 2020 GHMC elections may explain his thought process. For the GHMC elections, KCR changed candidates in about 40 wards to accommodate new candidates from other parties who joined the TRS. But the result did not favour the TRS, which lost at least 35 of the 40 wards where incumbents were dropped.

The TRS's corporator tally dropped from 99 in 2015 to 56 wards in 2023, a steep fall of 43 seats. On the other hand, the Bharatiya Janata Party, which had just four corporators in 2015, increased its tally by adding 44 wards in 2020.

Perhaps KCR did not wish for a scenario where MLAs would desert the party and add to the anti-incumbency mood if they found out they would not be considered in the 2023 elections. KCR decided to throw his weight behind the sitting legislators and possibly expected the people of Telangana to look at him and not the individual MLA candidates and elect the party to power.

During the campaign, KCR repeatedly appealed to the voters to see his work in the State since its formation and not worry about any other factor. KCR frequently highlighted Telangana's "dark phase" before 2014 and how the then chief ministers failed to bring in regional development. However, the voter did not believe in KCR this time.

Most voters in the State identified Telangana Rastra Samithi (TRS) as the Telangana party. In the 2014 General Election to the Telangana Assembly and the Lok Sabha, the 2018 State Assembly elections, and the 2019 Lok Sabha elections, the voters in Telangana stated that they would "Vote for Telangana" – making KCR's party synonymous with Telangana state. This goodwill among people for his party made KCR confident in ignoring all hints of anti-incumbency against legislators.

KCR's party had a deep-rooted connection with the people in its earlier avatar as the Telangana Rashtra Samithi. However, KCR had cut this umbilical cord when he renamed his party the Bharat Rashtra Samithi or BRS.

Ahead of the announcement of the name change, KCR spoke of how the Telangana model of development, which provides all necessities to most people in Telangana, must be replicated across the country. This idea was borne out of KCR's ambition to play a significant role in national politics, and if luck smiled on him, he possibly dreamt of becoming the Prime Minister.

However, shedding its Telangana identity came with a cost, as the party lost its sentimental value. The party also lost its right to criticise opposing forces outside the region as they tried to go national.

According to some insiders, KTR was not convinced about renaming the party to the BRS and fighting elections beyond Telangana state's boundaries. But he failed to stop his father, whom KTR addresses as 'sir' or 'boss', from making this decision, which is now widely considered disastrous.

The first hints about KCR's plans for national politics emerged after the Congress party's rout in the Assembly elections in five states in early 2022. In May 2022, he visited Chandigarh to honour soldiers who lost their lives in the Galwan Valley clash and farmers who succumbed during the year-long anti-farm law protests. Accompanied by Delhi Chief Minister Arvind Kejriwal and Punjab Chief Minister Bhagwant Singh Mann, KCR distributed Rs 3 lakh each to the families of the deceased farmers, fostering a strong pro-farmer image. His visit seemed a strategic step towards his national political aspirations, which became evident in KCR's subsequent call for "Ab Ki Baar, Kisan Sarkar". During this event, KCR emphasised the influential role of farmers in shaping governments, expressing hope that his pro-farmer stance would resonate across India.

A controversy, however, arose in November-December 2022 when reports of some cheques getting dishonoured appeared in the media. Chief Secretary Somesh Kumar clarified that 814 cheques were successfully encashed, while the remaining were not deposited within the three-month validity period.

In Telangana, the Congress party, BJP, and other parties criticised KCR for allegedly neglecting the families of 8,400 farmers who died by suicide in the State due to financial pressures. They accused KCR of diverting Telangana's resources to Punjab for political gains, a narrative which found resonance among a section of people.

Opposition parties, notably the Congress party, strongly criticised KCR on this matter. The Congress party accused KCR of reneging on his commitment to waive farmers' loans, a promise that contributed to his re-election for a second term in 2018.

According to the Congress party, KCR assumed office based on his pledge to waive farm loans amounting to Rs 20,389 crore. However, the banks did not waive these loans till May 2022. As farmers can get fresh loans from banks only when existing loans are paid, the Congress party asserted that due to the delay in KCR fulfilling his promise, farmers were compelled to obtain loans from private lenders at high interest rates.

One of the prime assets that KCR has is his oratory. His command of language and understanding of people's moods make him a legendary leader. It may not be an exaggeration if he thought he could convince people to vote for unpopular legislators. However, his health spoiled his political plans.

After announcing candidates ahead of other parties, KCR's ill health confined him to bed for two weeks after the Election Commission of India set the ball rolling for the elections. While the Congress party, emerging as the true challenger, took advantage of the 'golden period' in political canvassing, BRS leaders and cadres were waiting for KCR to hit the road.

While Congress party was surging ahead with a charismatic Revanth Reddy leading the charge, along with frequent visits of Rahul Gandhi and Priyanka Gandhi, the BRS had KTR and Harish Rao to fill in the void. The results suggest that KTR and Harish could not fill in for KCR, who ultimately managed to reach out to the voters across nearly 100 Assembly constituencies in Telangana.

One factor that has hurt both the BRS and the BJP was the perceived proximity between Chief Minister KCR and Prime Minister Narendra Modi. Many in Telangana believe KCR was soft in his attack on Modi or BJP. The Modi government's perceived inaction on Kavitha after she was questioned in the Delhi liquor policy scam strengthened the talk of KCR's proximity to the BJP.

Telangana Congress party leaders alleged that KCR was going soft on the Union government to protect his daughter from getting arrested despite high inflation and price rises. Rahul Gandhi's allegations against Modi and KCR resonated with certain sections of society. It made the BRS lose a certain percentage of Muslim voters.

While the BRS leaders project KCR as a 24x7 politician, people have bought into the opposition narrative that painted him as a leader who stays aloof and reclusive in his farmhouse. In support of their arguments, the opposition parties highlighted that KCR did not visit the State Secretariat between 2014 and 2018. Even after he built a new Secretariat complex, as the old one presumably had certain vastu defects, KCR only visited the Secretariat occasionally.

Another factor that seems to have cost the BRS badly was KCR's "arrogance". People enjoyed KCR's brash handling of those obstructing his speeches during public meetings till 2018, but during his second term, it was labelled as arrogance.

During his press conferences, KCR often came across as a leader who lacked patience and had a low sense of humour. While he used disrespectful words for others, he was found to be thin-skinned to any criticism. His short interactions with The Hindu newspaper's correspondent, Rahul Gandhi, whom I had known personally for many years, are widely used as memes. In the initial days, though journalists did not react aggressively to KCR's antics, they started responding differently in the last two to three years.

KCR's failure to fulfil the long-standing demand of journalists who sought housing plots, too, went against him when he required their support the most. A few senior journalists alleged that the KCR government even tried to bring in a split among the journalists on the lines of Telangana and Andhra. While many veteran journalists have been in the field for decades, few youngsters working in the TRS-owned media outlets tried to use their proximity to those in power and capture institutions like the Press Club, an act intensely disliked by journalists.

In 2023, the year of elections for the Telangana State Assembly, senior journalists, who are widely followed on social media, used the platforms to target KCR's style of governance. Many among these journalists, who are expected to stay neutral, were seen criticising or going to the extent of mocking KCR. The lack of extensive media support, which KCR enjoyed in the past, was another factor that hurt the BRS in Telangana.

Historically, predominantly landless and politically underrepresented Dalits have rallied behind KCR in Telangana, knocking out the TDP and the Congress party in the 2014 Assembly elections. However, after becoming the CM, Dalit activists claim that he has failed to fulfil his promises, such as making a Dalit the first Chief Minister of Telangana state and giving three acres of arable land to landless Dalit families. This failure had an adverse effect on their support for the BRS. Despite his failure, KCR passed the first major test in 2018 with flying colours. But by 2023, KCR did not enjoy similar popularity among them.

Ahead of the 2023 Assembly elections, he tried to win them over with the Dalit Bandhu scheme, but it hurt his party more. The scheme, where eligible SC families would receive Rs 10 lakh financial assistance, was shoddily implemented and became the Waterloo or KCR and his party. The BRS suffered losses in the seats reserved for Dalits.

Until the state's bifurcation, united Andhra Pradesh was predominantly ruled by the Congress party and, for about a decade, by the Telugu Desam Party. Dominant leaders from the Reddy and Kamma communities have always led these parties. However, after a decade of its rule, the TRS was labelled as a party led by a Velama (the community that KCR belongs to) while he was heavily relying on votes from Dalits.

DALIT BANDHU: KCR'S WATERLOO

The Dalit Bandhu scheme was launched in Huzurabad on a pilot basis in 2021. More than 18,000 beneficiaries were covered under the scheme. The scheme was extended to Chintakani (3,462), Tirumalagiri (2,223), Charagonda (1,407) and Nizamsagar (1,298) mandals in four different districts on saturation mode, which meant all eligible persons would benefit from the scheme. The scheme was then pared down, and the government rolled it out in two phases. The first phase, with a target of only 100 beneficiaries in each constituency, was completed in 33 districts, covering 11,837 beneficiaries in the state.

According to Telangana Scheduled Castes Co-op Development Corporation, around 38,600 Dalit families have benefited through the scheme so far, and the State had spent Rs 3,870.62 crore on the scheme as of 2023, including the first phase and pilot/saturation mode implementation before that.

Its second phase was announced in March this year. It aimed to identify 1,100 beneficiaries per constituency, nearly 1.3 lakh beneficiaries. However, the Dalit activists were unhappy with the progress of the second phase as they allege that KCR used it as yet another election promise whose implementation may wane even if the BRS returned to power.

According to the scheme's implementation guidelines, the district administration would finalise the beneficiaries based on the local MLA's recommendations. Depending on how they want to use the assistance, the beneficiaries are categorised into different sectors, such as agriculture, transport, manufacturing, retail, and services. A single unit under the scheme can comprise multiple sub-units within the same or different sectors. For instance, a unit may involve both dairy farming and poultry. In some cases, various beneficiaries can join to create a joint unit, with the project cost exceeding Rs 10 lakh. Several incidents have been reported where Dalits staged protests demanding transparent implementation of the scheme and alleged that beneficiaries on good terms with the MLA benefited majorly from the scheme. Activists alleged that in some constituencies, MLAs have sought about 30 per cent of the scheme amount as 'commission' in exchange for recommending the beneficiaries' names to the district collector.

In August 2023, alleging bias in selecting beneficiaries, a group of Dalits from Ankireddypally village in Kondapaka mandal of Siddipet district staged a protest. In October 2023, Dalits from three villages, Nerella, Jagadevpet, and Ramaiahpally in Jagtial district, staged a demonstration in front of the Panchayat office in Dharmapuri Mandal, alleging an unfair selection process due to recommendations.

According to a report by the Forum for Good Governance (FGG), in Vasalamarri, a village adopted by KCR, where the scheme was implemented in saturation mode, it was found that 75 people received benefits. Surprisingly, however, there were only 52 Dalit families in the village. The hurry to meet targets during this saturation mode meant that beneficiaries were given something by the district administration, which did not essentially help them. Amid the corruption allegations, KCR reportedly warned his party MLAs at the BRS plenary meeting in April 2023 against extorting money from Dalit Bandhu and the beneficiaries of the 2-BHK housing scheme.

Before the Dalit Bandhu scheme, the BRS, in its earlier avatar as the TRS, had promised three acres of land to Dalits in 2014. According to the Telangana government, there are approximately 18 lakh Dalit households. Under this land distribution scheme, three acres were supposed to be allocated to economically-disadvantaged SC women from the landless agricultural families.

The scheme carries a unit cost (one beneficiary) of Rs 21 lakh, with a maximum of Rs 7 lakh per acre. It included a comprehensive agricultural support package, with provisions for irrigation, seeds, cultivation costs, fertilisers, pesticides, among others for a single crop year, all funded by a 100 per cent subsidy to facilitate one year of crop assistance. The data on land distribution was only available until April 2018, when the government acquired 14,282.37 acres of land and distributed it to 5,607 beneficiaries.

As per the Telangana State Scheduled Caste Corporation, only 6,900 out of 18 lakh Dalit households received land between 2014 and 2023, with Rs 729 crore spent under the scheme over the past nine years.

FIRST SALVO

In the first week of April 2023, much before any possible winds of elections blew over Telangana, a claim made by a senior journalist increased the political temperature in the state.

Renowned journalist Rajdeep Sardesai, speaking in the "Neta Nagari" programme on *"The Lallantop"*, arguably India's most followed digital news platform, asserted that the Telangana Chief Minister K. Chandrashekhar Rao purportedly communicated to opposition parties his willingness to fund their entire Lok Sabha election campaign if he was chosen as the convenor for the opposition grouping. Rajdeep Sardesai reiterated this statement in his weekly video blog *"The Straight Bat"* on YouTube.

KCR might have hoped that the position of the convenor would propel him to the pole position of becoming the Prime Minister if the ruling NDA fell short of a majority and a coalition of opposition parties got a chance to form the next government.

KTR said that while he respected Rajdeep Sardesai, his comments were unexpected and uncalled for. He also refuted the claim that KCR wanted him to be declared the Prime Ministerial candidate to take on Modi. With no strong condemnation coming from the BRS, despite Sardesai's lack of concrete evidence, this claim generated significant attention.

The Congress party and the BJP utilised this opportunity to target the BRS and accused KCR and his family members of accumulating ill-gotten wealth. Parties opposing KCR claimed that he possessed wealth acquired through illegal means and propped up his daughter Kavitha's alleged ties with the "lobby" that was trying to manipulate the liquor policy in New Delhi to make a fortune. Social media and debates on a few regional media platforms trumpeted the possibility of another major scandal in Telangana. The first allegation is possible corruption in the Kaleshwaram Lift Irrigation Project.

No one can validate the veracity of Sardesai's claim. However, his remarks helped the Congress party and the BJP to weave a narrative that KCR and his family members have amassed enormous wealth and are ready to splurge it in the 2024 Lok Sabha elections.

KTR: HYDERABAD'S CHARMING PRINCE

In the 2014 elections, the Telangana Rashtra Samithi won only three seats in the Hyderabad city, or the region within the limits of ORR. These were the seats of Malkajgiri, Patancheru and Secunderabad constituencies. The remaining Assembly constituencies were won either by the Telugu Desam Party, which gained ground in the peripheral areas where a large number of voters had roots in Andhra Pradesh, or the Bharatiya Janata Party, which built for itself a considerable support base riding the wave of the Telangana movement. However, in the 2018 State Assembly elections, the voting pattern changed significantly, and the TRS won 15 seats in the same region within the ORR limits. One of the significant differentiators was Kalvakuntla Taraka Rama Rao, or KTR.

Charismatic, witty, knowledgeable and someone who could network with and attract global enterprises to invest in Telangana, KTR became Hyderabad's brand ambassador. His language skills made him a darling of the national media in Delhi. Everyone appreciated his Twitter interaction with followers and those in need.

He started his political journey as the son of KCR. However, he climbed up the political ladder quite quickly with his unique style of functioning and carved a niche for himself in regional as well as national politics.

Born on July 24, 1976, KTR served as the Minister for Municipal Administration and Urban Development, Industries, and Information Technology in the Telangana government. His early exposure to politics likely influenced his career choice. He pursued his education in the United States, earning a Bachelor's degree in microbiology and a Master's in Business Management. His educational background equipped him with scientific knowledge and managerial skills, which proved valuable in his later political career.

KTR officially entered politics in the early 2000s. His political foray began with his involvement in the Telangana movement alongside his father. His articulate communication skills and ability to connect with the youth played a crucial role in mobilising support for the cause. Over the years, KTR has taken on various responsibilities within the party.

His role in municipal administration and urban development has been pivotal in transforming the urban landscape of Telangana. Under his leadership, the State has witnessed a focus on infrastructure development, waste management, and the beautification of urban spaces. Initiatives like the "Swachh Hyderabad" campaign reflect his commitment to creating clean, sustainable urban environments.

The Comprehensive Road Maintenance Programme ensured that major thoroughfares were free of potholes and bad patches, once a persistent issue in the city.

As the Minister for Industries and Information Technology, KTR has been instrumental in attracting investments and fostering industrial growth in Telangana. The Telangana State Industrial policy, an initiative championed by KTR, aimed to simplify the industrial clearance process, making the State more business-friendly.

The absence of power cuts and the implementation of a free drinking water supply scheme were other factors that resonated positively with the people of Hyderabad in general, irrespective of where they held their voting rights.

Telangana's rise as an IT and business hub can be attributed, in part, to KTR's efforts to promote the State as an attractive destination for industries. KTR's emphasis on Information Technology extends beyond industrial growth; he has actively promoted the use of technology in governance, leading to initiatives like "T-Hub," a startup incubator that has gained national and international recognition. His vision for a tech-savvy and innovation-driven Telangana aligns with global trends and positions the State as a leader in the digital landscape.

The realty sector received a significant boost through the SRDP and Haritha Haaram projects, mainly concentrated in the western part of the city. This initiative endeared KTR to IT professionals.

The visual splendour in Hyderabad, enhanced by the newly-constructed State Secretariat, the Martyrs' Memorial and the colossal Ambedkar Statue, heightened the party's popularity among a section of the society. Rising real estate prices have become the yardstick for development in the public consciousness, overshadowing other issues.

While driving economic and technological advancements, KTR has also been committed to inclusive development. A multi-faceted approach to governance underscored his commitment to balanced and equitable development.

KTR's effectiveness as a leader is rooted in his administrative skills and ability to communicate with the public. He is known for his active presence on social media platforms, using them as tools for direct communication with the citizens. This approach fosters transparency and allows him to connect with the younger generation, a demographic that often plays a crucial role in shaping political landscapes.

KTR has faced his share of challenges and criticisms. Political opponents have raised concerns about governance transparency, land acquisitions, and the pace of development. However, KTR's ability to navigate these challenges and proactive approach to addressing public concerns have contributed to his sustained popularity.
KTR's political journey reflects an inherited legacy, educational prowess, and a commitment to progressive governance. His roles in urban development, industries, and information technology have contributed significantly to Telangana's transformation.

Over the past six years, there have been multiple theories on how, when, and why KTR would take the baton from KCR as the Chief Minister of Telangana. This argument picked steam after KTR was made the executive working president of the party in December 2018.

The residents of Hyderabad might have experienced a rude shock with the results of the Telangana State Assembly elections 2023. Insulated from people's mood beyond the Outer Ring Road, the people of Hyderabad would take a long time to come to terms with the change of guard in the state. Many young IT professionals use social media to express their fear of the future.

Even for those not bothered about the BRS losing the election, the realisation that KTR will no longer be the IT Minister or the Municipal Administration Minister has become unbearable.

KTR was one of the most significant factors that helped the BRS to win all seats in GHMC limits except the seven, which are considered traditional strongholds of the AIMIM, and that of Goshamahal, which has become a fiefdom of rabble-rousing Thakur Raja Singh Lodh.

Unlike previous instances where voter preference for a party might have stemmed from fear or despair, this time, it was an explicit acknowledgement of the work that promoted 'Brand Hyderabad' for investors. A day after the State Assembly election results and hours after KTR signed off, "#ITMinister "trended on social media platform X (formerly Twitter). Many netizens expressed concern over the void left behind by the charismatic KTR. Thousands took to various social media platforms to write their views on KTR and how he was essential for the progress Hyderabad was witnessing. Seeing this meltdown, the next IT Minister had big shoes to fill in.

While the BRS lost the majority in the 119 seats house, KTR retained his Sircilla seat with a margin of 29,687 votes, trouncing his nearest rival, K. K. Mahender Reddy of the Congress party, for the fifth time since 2009. In 2018, KTR defeated Mahender Reddy by a massive margin of 88,000 votes. In the 2023 Assembly elections, KTR polled 89,244 votes (47.28 per cent of the total), while Mahender Reddy got 59,557 votes (31.56 per cent). BJP's Rani Rudrama Reddy finished third with 18,328 votes (9.71 per cent). NOTA polled 842 votes, including two postal ballots.

Known as the "Textile Town of Telangana," Sircilla has long been renowned for its handloom and power loom industries, contributing significantly to the textile landscape of Telangana. KTR has been actively working on the economic development of Sircilla by promoting the textile industry and positioning the TRS as the party that champions local businesses and artisans.

Sircilla weavers benefitted hugely from the "Bhathukamma" sarees, which the government orders and buys from the local weavers. Despite being the most sought-after minister in the KCR cabinet, many fans of KTR in Sircilla believed he gave adequate time to the constituency, and the development witnessed in the town happened because of the efforts put in by KTR as a local representative and a minister.

In the run-up to the 2023 elections, a usually polite and thoughtful KTR turned brash. His statements on political opponents and his posts on social media before the counting day led to criticism online and offline. While addressing a public meeting in the Kamareddy Assembly Constituency, from where KCR contested, KTR ridiculed those contesting from the opposition parties. While KTR said Revanth Reddy and the Congress party would suffer a humiliating defeat, he not only failed to recall the BJP candidate's name but was quite dismissive about the candidate and his electoral prospects in Kamareddy. However, the results left KTR red-faced as the BJP's Katipally Venkata Ramana Reddy emerged as a double giant slayer, defeating an incumbent Chief

Minister, KCR and a prospective CM, Revanth Reddy.
On the day ahead of the results, KTR posted an image of him holding a gun with the caption, "Hattrick Loading 3.0. Get ready to celebrate, guys". However, the result had nothing to celebrate for KTR's party, and he became the target of trolling. He, however, reposted the earlier image and wrote, "This one ain't gonna age well. Missed the mark". Immediately, there was a flood of love from netizens for KTR on social media for gracefully accepting the defeat.

Addressing a press conference on the results day, KTR said that though the results were disappointing and unexpected, his party will accept the people's mandate and work towards playing a constructive role in the opposition benches. Congratulating the Congress party, KTR said that his party would give sufficient time to the party that won the elections to fulfil the election promises made to the voters before taking up the fight on behalf of the people.

HARISH RAO: KCR'S FIRE-FIGHTER

Harish Rao, a close member of the KCR family and a key speaker in the BRS, is another influential leader in Telangana politics. In 2023, Harish Rao was the only leader to win seven times as MLA on the 'car' symbol. He won with a thumping majority of 83,025 votes over his nearest rival, Congress party candidate Pujala Harikrishna. However, the margin was lesser than what he got in the previous three Assembly elections.

With KCR falling sick for two weeks after the election schedule was announced, Harish Rao shared the responsibility of touring Telangana and campaigning for the party with his cousin KTR.

Despite not campaigning full-time in his Siddipet Assembly Constituency, Harish Rao won the second-highest majority in the State in the elections. In contrast, BRS candidate K.P. Vivekananda Goud won with a majority of over 85,000 votes from Qutbullapur, which stood as the highest majority.

Modi & BJP

"Hit Wicket" is a rare occurrence in the world of cricket, and the Bharatiya Janata Party, under the current leadership of Narendra Modi, committing political suicide too is a rare occurrence! However, the saffron party's rise and fall in Telangana and how the party committed certain mistakes that snatched a defeat from an imminent victory in a case study for students of politics.

In the previous chapter, 'By-elections & Munugode', I elaborated on how the BJP gained momentum in the State after winning two bypolls between 2020 and 2021 and how it took an unwarranted risk in 2022 and suffered a considerable setback. This chapter will examine the BJP campaign led by and centred around Prime Minister Narendra Modi in 2023.

With the defeat in the Munugode bypolls and inaction against Kavitha, many political observers and party insiders dismissed the possibility of the BJP coming to power in the state. The BJP's decision to change its State unit president, Bandi Sanjay, and give prominence to Etela Rajender created an impression that the saffron party is working for the victory of the BRS to prevent the Congress party from winning the State Assembly elections. This perception spread like wildfire and became the most debated point in television discussions and between the people sitting in corner tea stalls across the length and breadth of the state.

In a major surprise, Narendra Modi, during a public meeting held at Nizamabad on October 3, 2023, said that the

Bharat Rashtra Samithi president and Telangana Chief Minister KCR had requested him to admit his party into the BJP-led National Democratic Alliance (NDA) in December 2020. In the public meeting, Modi recalled, KCR told him that he wanted to hand over the state's responsibility to his son KTR. KCR, Modi further recounted, sought his appointment for his son, who would come to Delhi to see him and seek blessings.

Modi added that he told KCR clearly that it is a democracy and he is not a king or an emperor to hand over the reins to his successor and that it is for the people of Telangana to decide whom to elect and whom to reject. This revelation by Modi affected the BRS campaign in elections because KTR and other party leaders had to clarify the party's stand, negating Modi's claims multiple times.

During one of his interviews, KTR even alleged that Prime Minister Modi was displaying blatant dishonesty, which is utterly disgraceful and condemnable. KTR further added that KCR is a fighter and would never join hands with a 'cheat' like Modi, who is also a liar. KTR even advised Modi, "The Prime Minister should try his hand at scriptwriting and has a good chance of winning the Oscar."

Referring to the Modi-led BJP as the country's most prominent 'junta and jumla factory', KTR said that a rabid dog did not bite the BRS leaders to lose their minds and join the NDA, which is a sinking ship. He also rubbished Modi's claims that the BRS funded the Congress party to fight elections in neighbouring Karnataka. He said if that was the case, why was the income tax department, which works under the Union finance ministry, not taking action?

While it was evident that certain social groups got inclined towards the Congress party this time, the ruling BRS and the BJP had their task cut out to prevent this surge in the vote bank for the grand old party of India. Scheduled Castes was one social group that the BJP chose to influence before the Telangana elections.

To prevent SCs or Dalits from backing the Congress party, Prime Minister Narendra Modi addressed a public meeting in Hyderabad on November 11, 2023, along with Manda Krishna Madiga, a prominent face among the SCs, who has been fighting for decades for the classification of SCs and the rights of the Madiga community under the banner Madiga Reservation Porata Samithi (MRPS).

When Krishna Madiga turned emotional during the meeting, the Prime Minister consoled him. Modi also assured the Madiga community of Telangana that he would fight on their behalf and stated that his government would work towards their betterment.

In his speech, Modi paid his respects to TN Sadalakshmi and TV Narayan, who fought for the rights of the Madiga community and recalled their sacrifices for the community's interests. Addressing Krishna Madiga as his younger brother and a friend, Modi praised his 30-year-old long efforts with the spirit of "One Life, One Mission".

Modi also apologised to the Madiga community on behalf of all political parties for betraying them after the

Independence and sought their forgiveness. He said the BJP has stood with the Madiga community in every struggle in the last three decades and is committed to ending this injustice as soon as possible. He assured the Madiga community that a committee would be formed to recommend ways for the Madiga empowerment.

Speaking about the long-drawn judicial battle on the issue of SC classification, which is in the Supreme Court, Modi said the Constitution that Baba Saheb Ambedkar drafted for the country has given him the responsibility to deliver justice, and the government of India would do its bit to ensure Madigas get justice in the top court.

Modi also took a jab at both the BRS and Congress parties and asked the people to be cautious of these parties. He alleged that the BRS is an anti-Dalit party and the Congress party is no less. While the BRS insulted Baba Saheb Ambedkar by demanding a new Constitution, the history of the Congress party is also similar. The Congress party, Modi alleged, opposed Baba Saheb and did not allow him to win the elections twice. The Congress party, he said, did not let the installation of Baba Saheb's photo in the Central Hall of the old Parliament for decades. Because of the Congress party, Baba Saheb was not even given a Bharat Ratna for decades.

On November 26, 2023, less than 72 hours before the campaign concluded, Modi raised pertinent questions about the KCR government. He attributed KCR's decision to contest from the second constituency to the BJP's candidate, Etela Rajender, who is contesting from Gajwel. Modi pointed to the discontent among farmers and the poor, citing the irrigation project named after Bhagwan Mallikarjun (Kaleshwaram) that has adversely affected the lives of many. Modi also accused KCR of neglecting the plight of those who lost their homes and lands due to the Kaleshwaram project.

The Prime Minister highlighted the significant efforts of the central government in constructing nearly two-and-a-half lakh houses in Telangana and alleged that thousands of these houses meant for the poor are yet to be handed over due to alleged unjust seizures by the State government. Modi assured that under a BJP government in Telangana, these houses would promptly reach the deserving beneficiaries, which is Modi's guarantee.

The Prime Minister announced the formation of the 'National Turmeric Board', a long-standing demand of turmeric farmers in the State. The Telangana BJP, aligning with this commitment, has pledged in its manifesto to transform Nizamabad into a 'Turmeric City' and confer a Geographical Indication (GI) tag to Armor turmeric, ensuring substantial benefits for Nirmal's turmeric farmers. This announcement was widely welcomed by the farmers of the erstwhile composite Nizamabad district, which produces the highest percentage of turmeric in the country.

On November 27, 2023, Prime Minister Modi addressed a public rally in Mahabubabad where he said that both KCR and the BRS realised the rising importance of the BJP and wished to ally with the saffron party. However, he rejected the proposal as he would never go against the wishes of the people of Telangana. Because of his rejection, Modi said a dejected KCR indulged in incessant criticism of him and his party.

From Mahabubabad, Modi travelled to Karimnagar, where he addressed another rally, in which he said Karimnagar is a testament to India's democratic traditions. He accused the Congress party of betraying its leaders, recalling alleged disrespect shown by the party to former prime minister P.V. Narasimha Rao, whose loyalty to the Congress party was unflinching."

For both the Congress party and the BRS, Modi said the 'family' comes first, and both of them "only have corrupt agendas, while the BJP aims to strive for the true empowerment of the people of Telangana".

The same day evening, the Prime Minister reached Hyderabad to hold his first-ever roadshow in the city. From RTC Crossroads to Narayanaguda, it was a sea of saffron with the BJP flags, Narendra Modi masks, baskets of marigold petals thrown in the air, and orange balloons.

All the lanes and the bylanes that meet the arterial road were closed for traffic from 1 pm onwards as double barricades were set up to create the corridor for the roadshow. The Narayanaguda and Chikkadpally Metro stations were closed, and passengers could not board or de-board the trains between 5 and 6 pm. Union Minister and Telangana BJP President G Kishan Reddy and BJP MP K Laxman also joined the Prime Minister for the roadshow, which witnessed an impressive crowd lined up on either side of the road and showering flowers on the vehicle.

As per the schedule, the Prime Minister was supposed to reach the RTC crossroads in the city by 4.55 p.m., but it was delayed by nearly 30 minutes. The city traffic police were on top gear that day, blocking traffic from all lanes to the main roads. It created a ripple effect on other routes, virtually making the city strand on roads for long durations. One aspect that caught everyone's attention was the presence of MRPS cadres during the roadshow.

With many top BJP leaders in Telangana, including the likes of Bandi Sanjay, Dharmapuri Arvind, and Etela Rajender, losing steam at a crucial hour, the entire responsibility of lifting the spirits of BJP cadres fell on the shoulders of Modi. The results of the Assembly elections were that the BJP won eight seats, seven of which came from Telangana's northern districts.

Raja Singh phenomenon

The lone survival or winner for the saffron party from the rest of the State was the hugely controversial Thakur Raja Singh Lodh, who till recently remained suspended from the BJP for his remarks against Muslims.

The election results for the Goshamahal Assembly segment, from where Raja Singh contested, underscore a substantial political shift towards the firebrand Hindu leaders who have faced challenges in the past few years. Not only was Raja Singh booked by the police multiple times for his hate speeches, but he was arrested on those charges. BJP leaders, cadres, and fans of Hindutva ideology allege that "the left-liberals and Islamists" ran a campaign against Raja Singh before the elections.

According to the Hindutva brigade, "Thakur Raja Singh urged the people in his political rally to support the businesses from the Hindu community. There have been previous reports that Islamists have urged the Muslim community to boycott Hindu businesses. For example, a video from 2019 where a Muslim leader urged his followers to make purchases only from Muslim businesses has gone viral on several occasions. What Singh said should be seen as a retaliation and not provocation."

Despite repeated warnings from the police and suspension from the party, Raju Singh did not switch to non-divisive politics. On November 17, 2023, a case was registered against Raja Singh for alleged hate speech at the Agarwal Bhavan in the Maharajgunj area of Hyderabad. The meeting was held on November 14, 2023, as a part of the BJP's election campaign.

According to the complainant, Raja Singh's speech during the meeting contained 'objectionable words', which could be heard and circulated via social media platforms. The speech available on the X platform of "Hindutva Watch" has Raja Singh allegedly saying, "The fight between love jihadis and Hindu daughters has been going on for years".

A complaint was registered claiming that such statements are highly objectionable and promote enmity between Hindus and Muslims, not just in Goshamahal but across the country. It is deeds like these that position Raja Singh among those politicians who have the highest number of criminal cases registered against them. In another video, Raja Singh was heard saying, "Whoever has a tilak on his forehead is my brother and a Hindu; I will befriend only people who sport a tilak. Our women, please do not become friends with burqa-wearing women. There was a time when Aftab threatened us, but now there is a threat from Ayesha. These are the Ayeshas who are introducing Hindu women to Aftabs."

During the election campaign, the vehicles that were covered with 'Vote for Raja Singh' banners on all sides played rhythmic slogans in support of the candidate. One slogan heard from the loudspeakers was "Thakur Raja Singh akele rashtrawadi neta hain jo aap aur aatankwadi ke beech ek sainik banke khada hain (the only nationalist soldier standing between you and terror elements)." I am sure such a slogan does not meet the Election Commission of India's guidelines. But did it come to its notice?

Raja Singh is usually given a hero-like welcome on almost every street he walks into. He is hailed as a hero by few because they say the Goshamahal Assembly segment, which has a sizeable migrant Hindu population, is surrounded by seven other constituencies that are dominated by the All India Majlis-e-Ittehadul Muslimeen (AIMIM) and the Hindus in Goshamahal see him as a "protector of Hinduism". As he entered narrow alleys, Raja Singh was welcomed with aarti thalis, flower petals were showered from the balconies, and it was common to hear young women scream "Raja bhaiya aaya hain, jaldi aao (Raja bhaiya has come, come quickly)" to their family members.

Lacklustre Campaign

The electioneering of the BRS and the Congress party has undoubtedly overshadowed that of the BJP, which appeared to be lagging in the absence of strong leadership across several constituencies. The most vocal among the BJP candidates came from the north Telangana districts, and the party lacked similar voices in the south Telangana districts.

The campaign in charge of the BJP candidates felt intense action on the part of the contesting candidates or the cadres when Prime Minister Narendra Modi or Union Home Minister Amit Shah visited the state; otherwise, there was inaction.

For example, the enthusiasm among the BJP cadres in the Dubbaka Constituency of Siddipet district, where the BJP's Raghunandan Rao handed out a shock defeat to the BRS candidate in the November 2020 by-polls, seemed waning in 2023.

Many local journalists observed that Raghunandan Rao's campaign, mainly undertaken on foot through villages and "thandas" (hamlets) through Dubbaka and Raipol mandals, did not receive great enthusiasm. The attack on BRS candidate Kotha Prabhakar Reddy with a knife, due to which he suffered injuries and was lodged at a hospital for at least two weeks, brought him sympathy, and this, too, had an impact on Raghunandan Rao's campaign. Despite Kotha Prabhakar Reddy recovering from a stabbing wound and missing in action, the campaign for him by the BRS leaders and workers appears to be energetic. KCR deputed his nephew and minister, Harish Rao, the Siddipet MLA, to spearhead the campaign in the constituency, which eventually helped the BRS candidate win.

According to some media reports, the BJP's campaign seemed to be lacklustre, drowned out by the BRS and Congress party's high-voltage electioneering. The BRS and the Congress party had more vehicles on the ground, fitted with posters of their leaders and candidates, playing various songs.
While Narendra Modi and Amit Shah visited Telangana multiple times to address rallies, other senior BJP central leaders, including party president J.P. Nadda and defence minister Rajnath Singh, have also campaigned. Closer to the elections, Uttar Pradesh Chief Minister Yogi Adityanath and Assam Chief Minister Himanta Biswa Sarma, known as fire-brand leaders, made whirlwind tours across constituencies, but it was possibly too late. The BJP candidates' campaigns were hamstrung due to the absence of known local party faces capable of drawing crowds and only depended on national personalities. Bandi Sanjay, contesting from the Karimnagar seat against minister Gangula Kamalakar, was mainly confined to his constituency and made few appearances elsewhere. Interestingly, Bandi Sanjay, like in 2018, once again lost in Karimnagar to Gangula Kamalakar.

Manifesto

The Bharatiya Janata Party, in its manifesto for the Telangana Assembly Election 2023, named "Sakala Janula Saubhagya Telangana - PM Modi's Guarantee", dealt with about 25 issues, which were mainly divided into 10 broad features. But, the party manifesto dodged freebies, which were announced by both the BRS and the Congress party in their respective manifestos.

The BJP's poll promises included abolishing four per cent reservation for Muslims in the state, a Backward Class Chief Minister, four free gas cylinders, relief from high petrol and diesel prices and setting up of an NRI ministry to help people from Telangana living in other countries.

The key points in the BJP manifesto are as follows:

1. The BJP promised to scrap the 4 per cent reservation accorded to the Muslims in the state. The party said it would instead increase the reservation quota for the Backward Class, Scheduled Castes (SC) and Scheduled Tribes (ST). Amit Shah said Telangana is the only State where Muslims are given "religious reservation" and promised to do away with the 4 per cent reservation accorded to the Muslims. He said his party would instead increase the reservation quota for the Backward Class, SCs, and STs."

2. The BJP further added that the beneficiaries of the Ujjwala Yojana will be given four gas cylinders per year for free.

3. The BJP also promised to implement the state's Uniform Civil Code (UCC). "Once the BJP forms government in Telangana, it will, within six months, bring the UCC in the state," Union Home Minister and BJP leader Amit Shah said.

4. The BJP promised a slew of benefits for the women. It said a fixed deposit worth ?2 lakh would be given on the birth of

a girl child, and the women's Self-Help Groups would be given loans only at a one per cent interest rate.

5. The party said the Hyderabad Liberation Day (on September 17) and the Razakar Vibhishika Smriti Divas (August 27) will "be celebrated officially by the government" once the BJP comes into power in the state.

6. Promising "zero-tolerance against corruption", Amit Shah said that once in power, the BJP-led government in Telangana will "investigate all the corruption cases through a system headed by the retired Supreme Court judge. All those involved in corruption will be made to stay behind bars."

7. The BJP said it will reduce petrol and diesel prices by slashing the Value Added Tax (VAT).

8. To support medium and small farmers, the BJP said it will provide them with financial assistance of ?2,500 per acre. Under the Pradhan Mantri Fasal Bima Yojana, the farmers will be given free insurance under the BJP government. Rice and paddy will be purchased at ?3,100 per quintal, and a market intervention fund for turmeric will be provided. It also promised MSP on parboiled rice and free of cost "fasal beema" under Pradhan Mantri Fasal Beema Yojna.
9. The BJP offered free laptops to those pursuing degree or professional courses and promised to provide jobs to 2.5 lakh youth in the State in the next five years.

10. The BJP also promised to solve the water dispute in the State with the help of the Krishna Water Dispute Tribunal.

Results: Deepening saffron hue

After winning eight seats, one in Hyderabad and the rest in northern Telangana, the BJP has doubled its vote share from just seven per cent in 2014 and 2018 to 14 per cent in 2023. The BJP contested 111 seats, and the party allocated eight seats to its alliance partner, Pawan Kalyan's Jana Sena Party (JSP). In the 110 seats BJP contested in 2018 and 2023, the party managed to increase its vote share in as many as 97 seats, which can be considered a major gain.

The biggest win for BJP was registered by rabble-rouser Thakur Raja Singh Lodh, who managed to increase his vote share from 45 per cent in 2018 to 54 per cent to retain the Goshamahal seat. Other seats where the party gained big are Nirmal (44 percentage points), Armur (31) and Sirpur (30), where the BJP candidates Alleti Maheshwar Reddy, Paidi Rakesh Reddy, and Palvai Harish Rao have won, respectively.

The BJP's vote share went up drastically in 12 other constituencies by 20 percentage points, including that of Huzurabad and Gajwel, from where former BRS minister Eatala Rajender contested on a BJP ticket, in Boath and Koratla, where BJP fielded its MPs Soyam Bapu Rao and Dharmapuri Arvind respectively, in Quthbullapur, LB Nagar and Secunderabad Cantonment segments in and around Hyderabad.

Dhanpal Suryanarayana Gupta in Nizamabad (Urban), Rama Rao Pawar in Mudhole, and Katipally Venkata Ramana Reddy in Kamareddy managed to increase the BJP vote share by more than 20 percentage points and win these seats. In areas with a considerably high Muslim population, like in Hyderabad, Rangareddy, Karimnagar, Nizamabad, Adilabad, and Nirmal districts, the BJP has either won or finished a close second.

Owaisis & Muslims

Muslims in Telangana, who constitute around 12.7 per cent of the electorate, have the clout to decide the destiny of political parties in at least 40 per cent of the 119 Assembly constituencies. While they are present in considerable numbers in almost all districts, they can play a decisive role in Hyderabad, Ranga Reddy, Mahabubnagar, Nalgonda, Medak, Nizamabad and Karimnagar districts.

According to the Telangana Social Development Report 2017, 17.13 lakh Muslims live in the Hyderabad district, constituting 43.5 per cent of the total Muslim population of 44.65 lakh in the state. The city has 24 Assembly seats, of which Muslim voters can swing the outcome in 10. Most Muslims of Hyderabad have resided in the Old City, the All India Majlis-e-Ittehadul Muslimeen (AIMIM) fief, for two decades. The party has consistently won all seven Assembly seats in the Old City.

The AIMIM is led by the Owaisi Brothers, who are counted among the country's most charismatic political figures today. An electoral legacy, which started with their grandfather Abdul Wahed Owaisi, who became the party president in the late 1950s and was carried forward by their father Salahuddin Owaisi, who won the Hyderabad Parliament seat six times in a row, rests on the shoulders of the two vociferous siblings.

The Owaisi Brothers, significantly the younger among the two, Akbaruddin Owaisi, often found themselves on the wrong side of acceptable norms. However, their political acumen and ability to grab the attention of the average voters is unparalleled in this part of the country. Elder brother Asaduddin Owaisi's speeches in the Lok Sabha and his addresses on various public and media platforms are heard with rapt attention by his fans and baiters alike. While Asaduddin Owaisi is known for his command over the Constitution and Indian legal framework, Akbaruddin Owaisi established Salar-e-Millat Educational Trust, which runs a chain of 'Owaisi School of Excellence' in Hyderabad, where free education is provided to children from weak economic background. The manner each of the seven AIMIM legislators and the party corporators have attended to the grievances of people from their constituencies, irrespective of their caste and religion, can be considered a best practice worth emulating in Indian politics.

The Owaisi Brothers were considered close to the Congress party during the times of the then Chief Minister Dr Y.S. Rajasekhara Reddy, who, via delimitation of Assembly segments in 2009, helped the AIMIM to expand its base from four or five seats to seven seats in the Old City of Hyderabad. Many political observers say that this unwritten pact between Dr YSR and the Owaisi Brothers ensured the latter batting for the Congress party in the seats beyond their fiefdom in the Old City. However, this camaraderie did not last long, and the stance taken by the last Chief Minister of united AP, Nallari Kiran Kumar Reddy, created a massive gap between the Owaisis and the Congress party.

The rift between the two parties has hurt the Congress party's prospects beyond Telangana a few times over the last decade.

Kiran Kumar Reddy, the Chief Minister of Andhra Pradesh from 2010 to 2014, wanted to assert his position in the State and, in the process, took steps that alienated the Owaisis completely. The rift widened after the Kiran Kumar Reddy government remained a mute spectator when certain Hindutva forces erected a canopy at the Bhagya Lakshmi temple, abutting the historic Charminar.

Following this, the speech made by Akbaruddin Owaisi on December 22, 2012, during a rally in Nirmal town of then Adilabad district, led to the complete severing of ties. In his speech, on which a case is still pending the courts, Akbaruddin denigrated Hindu gods and mocked traditions followed by Hindus, along with making controversial remarks against Hindutva groups. Akbaruddin was arrested in January 2013 and spent 40 days in prison before securing bail for himself.

When Akbar was in custody, his brother Asaduddin Owaisi was arrested by the Kiran Kumar Reddy government in a 2005 case of obstructing a government official. Asad's arrest sparked violence in the old city area, and this served as the last nail in the coffin and resulted in a complete breakaway of ties. This entire episode of Kiran Kumar Reddy vs the Owaisi Brothers occurred when the final phase of agitation for a separate Telangana State was in full swing.

Since the formation of Telangana, the Owaisi Brothers shared great camaraderie with the first Chief Minister of Telangana, KCR, whom Asaduddin Owaisi affectionately calls and encourages his followers to call mamu (uncle). Government policies like Shaadi Mubarak and Muslims getting benefits of various schemes have endeared KCR to the

Owaisi Brothers and the Muslims of Telangana alike.

This strong bond between them led to the Owaisi Brothers openly appealing to the Muslims of Telangana to vote in favour of TRS/BRS. According to some observers, the most significant benefit that KCR has done for the Muslims was the establishment of 200 residential schools and colleges exclusively for Muslims, where they are given free education, food and clothing up to Class 12. The TRS constantly claimed that there was not a single instance of communal violence in Telangana. The Old City, which used to witness curfews regularly during the Congress party regime, is peaceful now, and the Muslims are happy with TRS.

Buoyed with the electoral consolidation they achieved in Hyderabad, Asaduddin Owaisi, over the past decade, ventured into various states like Bihar, Uttar Pradesh, Maharashtra, and West Bengal, among others, where the AIMIM fielded candidates and even tasted success in a few. Whatever the outcome for the AIMIM, the Congress party and other so-called secular parties, which were hoping to be the natural claimants of Muslim votes, paid a heavy price due to the split in the votes. The Bharatiya Janata Party seemed to have gained electorally due to the split of votes in the opposition camp. The Owaisis did face a considerable backlash from "secular" groups or political outfits like the Samajwadi Party, the Rashtriya Janata Dal, and the Trinamool Congress, among others, along with the Congress party, for aiding the rise of the BJP electorally in India.

Irrespective of what happened in the other states prior to November 2023, the biggest test for Owaisis was once again in Telangana in the form of the State Assembly elections 2023. A growing anti-incumbency and perceived proximity between KCR and the BJP's top bosses had put TRS/BRS in a disadvantageous position in the polls.

The Owaisi Brothers had an uphill task in ensuring that their appeal to Muslims to vote for "mamu" was respected by the community. The biggest challenge before Owaisis was that they were not a considerable force beyond the old city limits, and they did not take part in elections in other districts of the state, barring very few wards in places like Bhainsa in Nizamabad. The election results proved that the Owaisis do not carry the clout beyond Hyderabad in general and beyond Old City in specific.

Result: Uncomfortable reality

After contesting in nine seats, AIMIM managed to retain the seven seats for the fourth consecutive time since 2009. But, looking into the data, we clearly understand that the Owaisis party lost a bit of its sheen in 2023. In 2018, the party fielded candidates in eight Assembly segments and garnered 5,61,089 votes or 2.7 per cent.

In the 2019 elections, despite contesting in an additional seat, the party's vote dropped to 5,19,379 or 2.22 per cent votes. A good 0.5 per cent vote drop speaks volumes about the party's challenge this time. This certainly does not indicate that the grip of Owaisis has weakened, but the numbers indeed suggest this was a peculiar election. In two of the seven Assembly segments it retained, the margin of victory of AIMIM candidates fell drastically, and these were the two seats where the party supreme, Asaduddin Owaisi, changed the candidates.

In Nampally, AIMIM's Mohammad Majid Hussain, former Mayor of Hyderabad, who was fighting an Assembly Election for the first time, won with a margin of 2,037 votes, over the Congress party's Mohammed Feroz Khan, whom many considered as a favourite from this seat. Yakutpura was another segment where the AIMIM candidate almost lost the election. Jaffer Hussain, who was shifted from his Nampally seat, where he would have faced tough competition from Feroz Khan, ran into an even tougher Amjed Ullah Khan of Majlis Bachao Tehreek and scrapped through a slender margin of just 878 votes.

In Jubilee Hills, where the Congress party fielded former India cricket captain and former parliament member Mohammed Azharuddin, the AIMIM candidate Mohammed Rashed Farazuddin got just 7,848 or 4.28 per cent of the votes. Maganti Gopinath of the BRS retained this seat with a majority of 16,337 votes, and the votes that the AIMIM candidate secured proved insignificant in all dimensions.

In the Rajendranagar Assembly Constituency, the AIMIM fielded a Hindu candidate, Mandagiri Swamy Yadav, who secured 25,670 or 7.82 per cent of the votes. This was a drop of 10.73 per cent of votes from the 2018 elections. Sitting MLA T. Prakash Goud of the BRS retained the seat with a margin of 32,096 votes over the BJP's Thokala Srinivas Reddy. While AIMIM here, too, remained an insignificant player, BJP gained almost 20 per cent of the votes from the last time.

Results of the other five seats where AIMIM candidates have registered comfortable victories, including Akbaruddin Owaisi from his traditional Chandrayangutta seat, are listed below:
The Congress party seemed to have gained extensively in the seats where Muslims reside in considerable numbers. This happened despite Asaduddin Owaisi appealing to Muslims to vote for *"mamu"* KCR.

In the Warangal West Assembly Constituency, Congress party candidate Naini Rajender Reddy registered a comfortable win with a margin of 15,331 votes over four-time Legislator Dasyam Vinay Bhaskar of the BRS. This seat, which comes under the Hanamkonda district, has over 60,000 registered Muslim voters, and a large section among them seemed to have voted for the Congress party candidate. The BJP's Rao Padma finished third with 30,826 or 18.46 per cent of votes.

Similarly, in Warangal East, which also falls under Hanamkonda district, Congress party candidate Konda Surekha won by a margin of 15,652 votes over the BJP's Errabelli Pradeep Kumar Rao. Surprisingly, incumbent MLA Nannapuneni Narendra lost 50 per cent of the votes he secured in 2018 and finished a distant third this time. Here, too, it's evident that Muslims have cast their vote in favour of the Congress party candidate.

In Mahabubnagar, where Muslim voters are considered to be over 150,000 or close to 3.5 per cent, the Congress party's Yennam Srinivas Reddy won over former minister and BRS candidate Srinivas V Goud by 18,738. The BJP's A.P. Mithun

Kumar Reddy finished a distant third with 19,919 votes or 11 per cent. It is results like these which suggest that the Muslims have voted in favour of the Congress party and not the BRS.

Another interesting Assembly segment to analyse is Khammam, which has close to one lakh Muslims. Both the Congress party and the BRS fielded candidates from the same caste, and the contest, as expected, remained two-sided, with a third candidate remaining insignificant. Here, the Congress party's Thummala Nageswara Rao registered a comfortable win over the BRS candidate Puvvada Ajay Kumar with a margin of close to 50,000 votes.

In Nalgonda, where Muslims are over a lakh, Komatireddy Venkat Reddy of the Congress party registered a big win over Kancharla Bhupal Reddy of the BRS with a close to 55,000 vote majority.

K. Shankaraiah in Shadnagar, Karireddy Narayan Reddy in Kalwakurthy, P Sudarshan Reddy in Bodhan, Rekulapally Bhoopathi Reddy in Nizamabad Rural, Makkan Singh Raj Thakur in Ramagundam among others are likely beneficiaries of Muslims votes shifting towards the Congress party.

The final reports suggest that 33 per cent of Muslims favoured KCR to continue, while 23 per cent wanted Revanth Reddy or the Congress party to come into power. This indicates a substantial section among the Muslims who expressed an independent view in the elections and were not carried over by any "calling".

In a press meet that Asaduddin Owaisi addressed on the day

of counting, he looked pensive and said his party would assess where it went wrong when it comes to specific seats like Yakutpura and Nampally and overall will determine the mood of people before the Parliament elections.

Two days after the Assembly sessions started under the new government, the AIMIM floor leader in the State Assembly, Akbaruddin Owaisi, expressed concern over not a single Muslim getting elected on the Congress party or the BRS tickets. The acrimony between the Congress party and the AIMIM will continue unless either of the two extends an olive branch to the other, a must for both before the General Elections in 2024.

Conceding defeat in the Telangana Assembly elections, Owaisi expressed his respect for the people's mandate and vowed to introspect on the party's shortcomings. He believed there had been significant development in Telangana under the leadership of KCR. However, he said people gave their mandate to the contrary, and the AIMIM will work on the loopholes and introspect this.

Seemandhra Dimension

Seemandhra is a composite word that refers to Rayalaseema as Seema and Coastal Andhra as Andhra. People of these two regions, which were not geographically close to Hyderabad, had a special affinity with the capital city. Casually called "Settlers", a term used in this book for the first and last time, have invested their lives in Hyderabad, and this city belongs to them as much as it belongs to those who call themselves Telanganites.

Since the 1950s, statehood has been a very emotive issue for both Seemandhra politicians calling for a Vishalandhra (Greater Andhra) incorporating all areas where people speak Telugu or for a section of politicians in Hyderabad State who argued against the composite Telugu State citing varying levels of development achieved in both regions.

A section of politicians used this sentiment in the 1960s to start the Mulki agitation, which snowballed into the Telangana movement. Seemandhra also witnessed a counter to the Telangana movement in the form of Jai Andhra agitation. The same emotion was used for the 2001 Telangana movement, which led to the creation of India's youngest state, Telangana.

People from the Seemandhra region, a part of the Madras Province of British India, claimed they had lost enough since independence, as it was often restructured. In 1953, when Telugu-speaking areas were carved out of the Madras province to create the Andhra state, Rayalaseema had to leave two Telugu-speaking taluks of Bellary to Karnataka. The entire Bellary district was previously considered a part of Rayalaseema, along with Kurnool, Ananthapur, Cuddapah, Chittoor and Nellore. The Telugu leaders also had to forsake their claim on Madras City, which had Telugu-speaking people in the majority. After the formation of Andhra Pradesh on a linguistic basis in 1956, parts of the East-Godavari region (Bhadrachalam and Nugur Venkatapuram Taluks) were merged with the Khammam district of Telangana region and Munagala of the Krishna district was merged with the Nalgonda district of Telangana region.

In 2014, Seemandhra lost Hyderabad city, the crown jewel of the united Andhra Pradesh. Though Hyderabad was not part of the Seemandhra region, it was the capital of the unified State since 1956. It was developed because of the efforts put in by people of all three regions of Telangana, Rayalaseema, and Coastal Andhra.

Even before 2014, Hyderabad contributed close to 50 per cent of the total revenue generated in Andhra Pradesh. Losing control of Hyderabad was the biggest setback for the people and politicians of the Seemandhra region. However, the maturity shown by all political parties, including the Telangana Rashtra Samithi, which led the separate Telangana agitation for more than a decade before 2014, ensured there was no bad blood between the people of the three regions. Those who came from Rayalaseema and Coastal Andhra regions for employment or business continued to live in harmony with those from Telangana, even after bifurcation.

Even a decade since Telangana state was formed, the bifurcation blues of the Telugu-speaking states are far from over. While there was no trouble in the people-to-people connection, politics never let the situation settle down.

In December 2022, the Andhra Pradesh government moved the Supreme Court of India, seeking the division of assets between Andhra Pradesh and Telangana. It sought a fair, equitable, and expeditious division of assets and liabilities. The AP government has pegged the value of undivided assets at Rs 143 lakh crore and claimed that as many as 91 institutions are included in Schedule IX, 142 institutions are in Schedule X, and 12 institutions have not found a place in either of the schedules.

As 91 per cent of the total institutions are located in Telangana, non-division of assets will be a loss to Andhra Pradesh. It will also harm the rights of people and about 1,59,000 employees working in these institutions. On January 9, 2023, the Supreme Court asked both the Central and Telangana governments to respond to the petition. But no final resolution was made until this book had gone for print. The total value of the fixed assets of the 245 institutions to be divided is about Rs 1,42,60,100 crore.

The prospects of a resolution repeatedly brightened with its inclusion in the agenda of pending interstate issues with Telangana by the Union home ministry. A Dispute Resolution Committee was constituted, with the Union home secretary as the chairman and the chief secretaries of both states as members. The committee has held several meetings but without any positive outcome. Against this background, asset bifurcation and resolution of other issues between the two states simmer whenever elections are held in Telangana or Andhra Pradesh.

Telangana has at least 25 Assembly segments, where people who originally hailed from Rayalaseema and Coastal Andhra regions are a deciding factor. While there are segments like Secunderabad and Malkajgiri in which people who originally hailed from Kerala and Tamil Nadu, and segments like Goshamahal, where those who originally hailed from north Indian states have a considerable say, those hailing from the current Andhra Pradesh districts form a substantial chunk.

In addition to all other communities, those belonging to Kamma and Kapu castes include the most vocal and numerically influential grouping. According to an estimate based on the Telangana government's integrated household survey, the population of those having their origins in Andhra Pradesh in the GHMC area is 58 per cent. In the undivided Ranga Reddy, Medak, Warangal, Nizamabad and Nalgonda districts, their population is about 53 per cent. In areas like Kukatpally, Lingampally, LB Nagar, Musheerabad, Patancheru, Quthbullapur, Malkajgiri, Medchal and Uppal, the percentage of the population who hailed from AP regions is 58.5.

In the constituencies where the people of Seemaandhra origin are in more significant numbers, those belonging to the Kamma caste are the deciding factor only in some constituencies. Those from the Kapu, Brahmin and other castes hold the key in different constituencies. For example, the Kamma population in the Banswada Constituency is about 45,000, and 30,000 in Nizamabad Rural and 23,000 in

Bodhan, both in the Nizamabad district. Kodad in Nalgonda district has about 30,000 people from the Kamma community. In the Malkajgiri Lok Sabha Constituency, the Brahmin community has a dominant 85,000 population. In Kukatpally, the Kapu community has 1.6 lakh members. In some constituencies, more than one caste is dominant.

LB Nagar has about 3 lakh people from the Kamma and Brahmin communities. In Serilimgampally, voters from the Kamma community dominate the 2.5-lakh-strong electorate of non-TS origin. In Quthbullapur, the 2.5-lakh 'Seemandhra' community is dominated by Kshatriyas and those from the Backward Castes. In Patancheru, Kapu, Kamma, and Brahmin communities, voters form a dominant part of the 75,000 people with Seemandhra origins. In Sanathnagar, the 50,000 voters mainly comprise the Kamma, Kapu and Backward Classes.

Given the strength of people with Seemandhra roots in Telangana, political developments in Andhra Pradesh resonate in Telangana as they happened before the 2023 Assembly elections. The arrest of Telugu Desam Party chief and former chief minister Nara Chandrababu Naidu influenced Telangana politics. Though the TDP pulled out of the election fray in Telangana, its followers in the State ensured their statements and actions were taken seriously by the BRS and the Congress party.

Just months before the Telangana Assembly polls, Telangana IT minister and BRS working president KTR turned down a request from Nara Lokesh, the TDP general secretary and son of Nara Chandrababu Naidu, for permission to conduct rallies in the Hyderabad IT Hub in support of his jailed father.

KTR said Lokesh approached him after police began a crack-down on demonstrations and protests organised by the TDP in the IT corridor of Hyderabad. However, he declined the request, stating that the protests were not allowed in the IT hub even during the Telangana movement and asserted that the IT industry should not be disturbed.

KTR said the arrest of Chandrababu Naidu was primarily a political move and a battle of wits between two rival political parties in the state, which had nothing to do with Telangana and its people. Hence, Telangana will not get dragged into what happens in Karnataka, Tamil Nadu, Andhra Pradesh, and Chhattisgarh because that is of no consequence. KTR said, "If someone wants a nautanki (drama) here, I only have to say that we don't want to be part of nautanki (drama), and it would be like Begaani shadi mein Abdullah diwana (Abdullah has gone mad with enthusiasm over a stranger's wedding)."

KTR's nonchalant remarks did not go down well with TDP admirers in Hyderabad. Expressing anguish over the attitude of KTR, many youngsters belonging to the Kamma community took to social media to express their resolve to prove that they matter in Telangana politics and extended support to the Congress party.

Some posts on social media read, the "BRS is ideologically hostile to Kammas, and Kammas were projected as enemies of Telangana during the agitation for a separate state. The Congress party appears to be the only alternative in

Telangana, and PCC chief Revanth Reddy appears more accommodating than KCR or KTR."

In Telangana, Backward Castes, Scheduled Castes, Scheduled Tribes, and minorities constitute over 85 per cent of the population. The exact percentage is unknown because we do not have a reliable caste census or had no census since 2011. The Telugu Desam Party had a tremendous following on caste lines, and this is where KTR and his BRS faltered.

Though the BRS fared well in the constituencies where the party fielded candidates belonging to the Kamma community, the narrative on social media emerged as a significant cause of worry for the BRS.
Though the people of Telangana, Rayalaseema, and Coastal Andhra had never gone to each other's throats, politics kept them divided on regional sentiments. Unfortunately, the two sister states of Telangana and Andhra Pradesh still have disputes over numerous pending administrative matters, and they get raked by politicians at their convenience. The Andhra Pradesh government raked up a similar issue on the poll day in Telangana.

In the wee hours of November 30, 2023, just hours before voting for the Telangana Assembly elections was to begin, a large contingent of around 500 armed personnel of the Andhra Pradesh police bulldozed a gate of the Nagarjuna Sagar dam on the Krishna River, which flows between the two states, occupied the dam infrastructure and released water from the reservoir towards Andhra Pradesh. As per the Andhra Pradesh Reorganisation Act, 2014, the operational control of the Nagarjuna Sagar Dam over the Krishna River, which straddles the districts of Nalgonda in Telangana and Palnadu in Andhra Pradesh, is with the Telangana government.

A First Information Report (FIR) registered by the Telangana police on this issue stated that at 2.03 am, Andhra Pradesh police personnel attacked the gate on the right bank, on the side of Andhra, which is under the control of the Telangana Irrigation and Command Area Development (CAD) Department. Around 500 armed personnel bulldozed the gate and allegedly trespassed on the dam. They laid barbed wire fencing, took possession of the dam from sluice gates 13 to 26, and took control of the right canal head regulator and right bank connectivity by violating the existing system. They also broke four CCTV cameras. Gates 13 to 26 are for releasing water to Andhra Pradesh.

Farmers in Andhra Pradesh, which is downstream of the dam, have been demanding the release of water from the dam. On the day of the incident, AP irrigation minister Ambati Rambabu said that water was not being released to AP, and the State had only taken its rightful share of 66 per cent of the water.

Even as the Telangana Police registered a case against Andhra police for alleged trespass on the dam, Telangana Pradesh Congress Committee chief Revanth Reddy put a political spin on the incident, claiming that it was "staged" to rouse the sentiments of Telangana voters ahead of polling. But the average voter did not react to this episode, and polling went ahead in Telangana unhindered.

Another interesting aspect of this Seemandhra dimension in Telangana State Assembly elections is that many people living in Visakhapatnam and other parts of AP travelled to Telangana to exercise their adult franchise here, as they are registered voters in this state.

Assembly segment	Winner	Party	Votes	%	Runner-up	Party	Votes	%	Margin
Malakpet	Ahmed Balala	AIMIM	55,805	42.27	Shaik Akbar	INC	29,699	22.50	26,106
Nampally	Md Majid Hussain	AIMIM	62,185	40.83	Md Feroz Khan	INC	60,148	39.49	2,037
Karwan	Kausar Mohiuddin	AIMIM	83,388	47.42	Amar Singh	BJP	41,402	23.55	41,986
Charminar	Mir Zulfeqar Ali	AIMIM	49,103	50.05	Megha Rani Agarwal	BJP	26,250	26.76	22,853
Chandrayan gutta	Akbaruddin Owaisi	AIMIM	99,776	64.89	Muppi Seetharam Reddy	BRS	18,116	11.78	81,660
Yakutpura	Jaffer Hussain	AIMIM	46,153	32.86	Amjed Ullah Khan	MBT	45,275	32.24	878
Bahadurpura Mubeen	Mohammed	AIMIM	89,451	62.24	Mir Inayath Ali Baqri	BRS	22,426	15.60	67,025

According to some reports, at least 5,000 people travelled to Telangana from Andhra Pradesh to cast their vote. These included those in public sector units like Hindustan Petroleum's Visakha refinery, Rashtriya Ispat Nigam's Visakhapatnam Steel Plant, Visakhapatnam Special Economic Zone, Central government organisations like the Eastern Naval Command, and the Indian Institute of Management at Visakhapatnam, along with many others working in several private sector organisations. Interestingly, the people living beyond the boundaries of Telangana had a say in the political fortunes of the MLA contestants in the state.

After the Telangana State Assembly elections, a controversy broke in Andhra Pradesh, with the YSR Congress alleging and even lodging an official complaint over the alleged enrolment of Telangana voters in the neighbouring state. The leaders of the YSR Congress claimed that the enrollment of such people violated Section 17 of the Representation of People's Act 1950, which prohibits the registration of one person in more than one constituency.

Andhra Pradesh social welfare minister Merugu Nagarjuna, AP Planning Board vice-chairman Malladi Vishnu, and MLC Lella Appi Reddy complained to the State chief electoral officer Mukesh Meena with evidence at the AP Secretariat in Velagapudi. The YSR Congress party has alleged that the Telugu Desam Party has violated electoral norms and conducted a new voter registration and voter verification drive in Hyderabad immediately after the Telangana Assembly election results were declared.

People of Interest

Chief Minister K. Chandrashekhar Rao was the most essential character in the Telangana State Assembly elections; his prime challenger and subsequent victor, Revanth Reddy, was the second most important face. Apart from them, several prominent individuals, such as KTR and Harish Rao from the BRS, Bandi Sanjay and Etela Rajender from the BJP and a few other established leaders from the Congress party, played important roles in the elections. Nevertheless, there was a set of people who were not in the election fray directly but played a decisive role in the election outcome. Here are brief profiles of them.

Y.S. Sharmila Reddy

Yeduguri Sandinti Sharmila Reddy (born December 17, 1974), popularly known as Y.S. Sharmila or Y.S. Sharmila Reddy or YSSR, is the founder and president of the YSR Telangana Party (YSRTP). She is the younger sister of Andhra Pradesh Chief Minister Y.S. Jagan Mohan Reddy and the daughter of late Dr Y.S. Rajasekhara Reddy, the former chief minister of united Andhra Pradesh, and Y.S. Vijayamma. Before venturing into Telangana politics, she was the convener of the YSR Congress Party. Sharmila Reddy first made headlines after campaigning for the YSR Congress in the absence of her elder brother, Jaganmohan Reddy, in June 2012 in Andhra Pradesh.

The YSRCP won 15 of the 18 Assembly seats and one Lok

Sabha seat for which the by-elections were held between 2012 and 2014. Sharmila Reddy began her 3,000-km padayatra (walkathon) at Idupulapaya in Kadapa district on October 18, 2012, and completed it on August 4, 2013, in Ichchapuram in Srikakulam district, covering 14 districts of united Andhra Pradesh.

Before the 2019 Andhra Pradesh State Legislative Assembly elections, Sharmila undertook an 11-day bus yatra across Andhra Pradesh in branded buses with a "Bye Bye Babu" timer clock, suggesting that time was up for the then chief minister Nara Chandrababu Naidu. The "Praja Theerpu - Bye Bye Babu" campaign covered 1,553 kilometres and addressed 39 massive public meetings.

On April 9, 2021, Sharmila Reddy announced her intent to form a new political party focusing on Telangana. A couple of months later, the YSR Telangana Party took birth on July 8, 2021, the birth anniversary of her late father Dr Rajasekhara Reddy. She undertook "Praja Prasthanam Padayatra" under the banner of the YSR Telangana Party and completed 3,800 km of padayatra covering all districts in Telangana.

The people appreciated her sharp attack on MLAs over corruption, adding to the growing anti-incumbency against the KCR regime. Sharmila Reddy's popularity rose to great heights in the second half of 2022 when her car was towed away by traffic police with the help of a crane, even as she sat inside it in protest against the Telangana Chief Minister. These visuals went viral internationally, and media worldwide highlighted this news.

Despite her soaring popularity, Sharmila Reddy, in November 2023, declared that her party would abstain from participating in the Telangana Assembly elections, acknowledging the electoral potential for the Congress party. She also said that her aim was not to undermine the Congress party but to pledge her support if the Congress party were to assume power, ensuring the successful implementation of their policies.

In a letter to Rahul Gandhi, Sharmila Reddy stated, "In scripting the imminent defeat of the BRS, it is felt that Congress party stands a chance, and any division of anti-incumbency votes at this stage will be a hurdle in dethroning KCR. As per many surveys and ground reports, it is established that our participation in the Assembly elections will directly impact the vote share of the Congress party in many constituencies. Therefore, the YSR Telangana Party has decided to withdraw and not contest the Telangana Assembly elections. I have made this important decision for the state's larger interest and to ensure the bigger cause of people. The YSR Telangana Party extends unconditional support to the Congress party. We urge all the YSR Telangana Party leaders, cadres, and all YSR fans to join forces and strengthen the Congress party at this crucial juncture for a better Telangana. I pray and wish the Congress party does well in the upcoming elections."

During her Praja Prasthanam Padayatra, Sharmila Reddy faced hurdles at every step of her path. She focused on enlightening people about their rights and what they deserve. In the process, the YSSR attacked the local legislators for their misdeeds. Once her popularity started rising in 2022, those in power tried to contain her. It was interesting to note that every legislator who ridiculed, abused, and accused YSSR lost in the 2023 elections.

Prominent names like Singireddy Niranjan Reddy, Peddireddy Sudharshan Reddy, Puvvada Ajay Kumar, Guvvala Balaraju, Balka Suman, from the BRS, Turupu Jayaprakash Reddy aka Jagga Reddy of the Congress party, and even Tammineni Veerabhadram of the CPI(M) have lost miserably from their respective seats. On the other side, those who welcomed the YSSR for her efforts have all won, like Nalamada Uttam Kumar Reddy, Komatireddy Venkat Reddy, Bhatti Vikramarkha Mallu, and even Kunamneni Sambasiva Rao of the CPI.

Disclosure: Starting in the last week of August 2022, a small team of Nitin Tanksale, Pavan Nanduri, Sreekar Reddy, and I have been associated with YSSR's Praja Prasthanam Padayatra. We gave her suggestions on the on-ground activities and managed national media relations. We travelled with her several times across various districts and to the national capital. Working with YSSR was a unique experience, and her grit to excel is contagious.

R.S. Praveen Kumar

Dr Repalle Shiva Praveen Kumar (born November 23 1967), popularly known as RSP, is a former officer of the Indian Police Service (IPS) who served as the secretary of the Telangana Social Welfare Residential Educational Institutions Society and the Telangana Tribal Welfare

Residential Educational Institutions Society. RSP was a recipient of the President's Police Medal for meritorious and was also awarded the Telangana Excellence Award by the government of Telangana on the eve of the 71st India's Independence Day.

During his career, RSP introduced the "P5 Model" into the Social Welfare Residential Schools and added several innovative and path-breaking programmes like e-Plus Clubs, Voice for Girls, horse riding, filmmaking, music, dance, water sports, mountaineering, Ignitor, W Plus Clubs, Impact, among others, for holistic development of the children.

During his tenure at TSWREI, students successfully launched two payloads, Swaero Sat 1 and Swaero Sat 2. into space The Swaero Sat-1 was designed to study cosmic radiation and ozone layer concentration at various altitudes. The Swaero Sat 2 is an experimental payload that looks at atmospheric pollutants like methane gas, carbon monoxide, radiation, and temperature levels.

RSP started SWAEROES, an acronym for Social Welfare Aeroes (Greek for sky); it means that the sky is the limit, and there is no reverse gear, no looking back or no slowing down. Swaeroes students are focused on academics and success in arts, cultural programs, sports and games. Springer Publications, a leading international scientific publishing company that publishes over 1,200 journals and more than 3,000 new books annually, has published the work of Praveen Kumar in its series 'Empowering Teachers to Build a Better World'. His work is selected as one of the six nations shortlisted worldwide.

After resigning from his government job, RSP joined the Bahujan Samaj Party "with a calling" that it was time "Dalits and Bahujans strive to achieve political power" in the state. And Swaeroes formed the backbone of his political ambitions. The nomination of RSP from the Sirpur Constituency made Sirpur a point of discussion for the first time in its electoral history. The BSP, too, got unprecedented visibility due to RSP joining the party and taking the electoral plunge. Sirpur is the first Assembly Constituency of Telangana and shares its borders with Maharashtra and a Phule-Ambedkarite consciousness.

In March 2021, a video went viral during an oath ceremony of a Swaero movement held at Dhulikatta Buddhist Shrine in Peddapalli district. In the video, Praveen Kumar was seen repeating "Buddha Vandanam" vows taken by Dr Ambedkar when he converted to Buddhism, which included denouncing faith in certain Hindu gods. The video was circulated, and right-wing groups criticised him.

Telangana BJP politicians and Vishva Hindu Parishad members accused him of spreading sentiments against Hinduism among students using the Swaero movement. Praveen Kumar defended against the accusations and issued a statement saying Swaeroism is an inclusive ideology and they don't teach any prejudice against any religion. The statement also stated that they work for a just and equal society in the country only through education, health awareness, scientific thinking and economic empowerment, not through hatred.

Despite a vigorous campaign for two years, RSP lost from the Sirpur Constituency, finished third and secured 44,646 votes. His opponents, the BJP's Dr. Palvai Harish Rao, who won the election, polled 63,302 votes, and the BRS' Koneru Konappa polled 60,379. Not just RSP but the Bahujan Samaj Party has faced a poll debacle, and the party registered less than 1.5 per cent of the total votes polled in the state. This result indicated that the BSP support base has not translated into votes, and even in the Scheduled Castes and Scheduled Tribes reserved segments, the party has not made any significant performance.

Shireesha aka Barrelakka

A Group-1 aspirant, Karne Shireesha, was the most prominent among the independent candidates who contested in the Telangana Assembly elections in 2023. A video that Shireesha shot of herself on her mobile changed this young girl's life forever. Though the video turned into a nightmare in the initial phase, it subsequently catapulted her into an aspirational figure for the underprivileged.

Shireesha cleared the Telangana State Public Service Commission's Group I preliminary exam twice after it was cancelled initially and held again due to the question paper leak. The Group II exam, too, was postponed, and there was no clue about the Group III and IV exams. It was here that the life of this articulate woman took a turn as she returned to her village frustrated over the delay in the issue of job notifications and frequent question paper leaks that brought to nought all preparations of job aspirants.

Back in the village, Shireesha purchased four buffaloes with the help of her mother after the latter insisted that she get married and lead a simple life as a village folk. She inadvertently took a video of herself one day while herding the animals.

She posted it on YouTube with comments criticising the government and narrating the plight of unemployed youth. This attracted nearly nine lakh followers for Shireesha on YouTube, Instagram and Facebook. With her post going viral and evoking solid responses from unemployed youth, their families, and people in general, the police booked a case against Shireesha under Section 505 (2) of IPC. As a result, she was frequently summoned to the court and the police station. This video got her the moniker "Barrelakka" (buffalo sister), but we will go with her original name here.

Felt harassed by the system, Shireesha filed a nomination to contest in the Assembly election as an independent candidate to assert herself from her native Kollapur Assembly Constituency. This made contestants of mainstream parties sit up and take notice of her as support for her swelled each day. Her opponents included former minister Jupally Krishna Rao of the Congress party and then incumbent BRS MLA B. Harshavardhan Reddy. She was among 14 candidates in the fray.

Looking at the swelling support and prominence of Shireesha, the rivals mounted pressure on her to withdraw, but she refused as she grew in confidence. Her mother also wanted her to withdraw because a lot of money was needed to fight elections. Shireesha received threatening calls, which culminated in an attack on her brother Chintu.

She recounted the incident in a video and moved the

Telangana High Court, which awarded her police security. If she withdrew, Shireesha was offered money, a house, and even an agricultural plot by political parties. But nothing shook her strong will to fight the election, which was the means to highlight the plight of the unemployed youth in the state. During the campaign phase, Shireesha recalled that the Dharani portal of the government on land transactions was a curse to people with low incomes, and her family lost its roadside land of 10 guntas (1,012 square metres) as some persons offered his father binges of drink and forged his signatures on plain paper to complete the transaction on Dharani.

Shireesha was overwhelmed by the support and the donations she received. But she was happy with the support from the volunteers, whom she did not know but had travelled from various parts of Telangana and Andhra Pradesh, stayed on the roadside, yet helped Shireesha in her campaign. Love and affection that Shireesha got from people cannot be purchased by spending lakhs. She was gifted a car and Rs 7 lakh by donors, including a former Puducherry minister, Malladi Krishna Rao. A former CBI joint director, V.V. Laxminarayana, participated in her door-to-door campaign for her, and filmmaker Ramgopal Varma extended moral support on social media. Actor and Jana Sena Party chief Pawan Kalyan also supported her. Shireesha's large team of supporters rounded off nearby villages as part of the campaign by making instant decisions on their destination depending on inputs about the availability of villagers.

From beyond the borders of Telangana, the Andhra Pradesh Unemployed Youth Joint Action Committee extended support to Shireesha. Several youths staged a support demonstration near the public library in Visakhapatnam in her support. They claimed that Shireesha's nomination questions the tall claims often made by political class over development and employment creation.

Visakhapatnam's youth requested that Kollapur voters vote in favour of Shireesha and said only the youth can bring a positive change in the country. Some youth organisations even stated that political parties, at least those in the opposition, should have accommodated about 10 unemployed youth by giving them tickets to contest in the elections, and this would have displayed their sincerity and commitment towards helping the unemployed.

Shireesha garnered just 5,754 votes in the election, in which Congress party candidate Jupally Krishna Rao had a margin of around 29,000 votes over the BRS's Harshavardhan Reddy. Despite her loss, Shireesha will be remembered for a long time for her decision to contest in the elections and not back off despite the hardships and threats she and her family faced. She will motivate youth who wish to stand up against the system. Shireesha and many like her are credited for highlighting the apathy of the BRS government and deserve credit for the result.

Pawan Kalyan

Maverick Pawana Kalyan, aka PK, was another interesting character in the Telangana Assembly elections. He did not contest the polls but fielded eight candidates on Jana Sena Party (JSP) tickets. These eight candidates contested in alliance with the Bharatiya Janata Party, the third blunder the saffron party committed in the elections. Pawan Kalyan, the lone alliance partner to the party in power in Delhi from the Telugu states, proved to be a disaster in Telangana.

While the JSP had initially intended to contest in 32 seats and announced the names of Assembly segments from where it would field candidates, the number got trimmed to just eight after a meeting between Pawan Kalyan and Amit Shah, taking into consideration the JSP's ability to swing votes and ease the BJP's burden of finding and fielding winnable candidates.

The eight seats in which the JSP fielded candidates were Khammam, Kothgudem, Wyra, Aswaraopeta, Kukatpally, Tandur, Kodad, and Nagarkurnool. While the BJP had limited clout in Khammam and Mahbubnagar districts, the party's choice to give away the Kukatpally seat to the JSP was a big surprise to political pundits. Even BJP cadres in Kukatpally opposed this party's decision, and it was reported that forging a synergy between the two parties was very difficult.

The JSP fielded three backward class candidates from the eight seats it contested. It added to the narrative of the BJP, which announced to have given priority to BC candidates and also promised a BC MLA as the Chief Minister if the party came to power in Telangana. The BJP-JSP alliance fielded 39 BC candidates, which allowed the State unit president, Kishan Reddy, to claim that his party fielded a maximum of BC candidates against the Congress party's 22 BC candidates and the BRS' 23 BC candidates.

Pawan Kalyan, making his maiden political foray into Telangana after a decade, shared the stage with Prime Minister Narendra Modi during a public meeting in Hyderabad. In this meeting, PK praised Narendra Modi as a visionary and even stated that the PM would make decisions only for the country's best interest and not for electoral gains.

His claim that revoking Article 370 in Kashmir was not done for electoral gains was scoffed at by political analysts and the media. Some analysts termed it the political ignorance of Pawan Kalyan, who was recently considered a "part-time politician" in Andhra Pradesh and had no presence in Telangana.

During the campaign, PK once said he was saddened by the level of corruption in Telangana, as confessed by a contractor in a television interview, and said people of the State deserve corruption-free governance.

While he toured constituencies where the JSP candidates were in the fray, PK chose the last day of the campaign to hold a roadshow in Hyderabad's Kukatpally area. During this roadshow, Pawan Kalyan said the JSP stayed away from the electoral fray in Telangana in deference to the people's wishes.

Though the party only participated in agitations, after repeated requests from the people, the JSP has entered into electoral fray in Telangana, and assured to work for the benefit of all communities. PK stated that Telangana had endured loot during the Jala Yagnam scheme of Dr Rajashekar Reddy and alleged that the conditions in

Telangana were the same now. The youth in the State were depressed and dejected.

Despite his last-minute pitch and best efforts, all eight JSP candidates lost their deposits. Many analysts feel that this drubbing of the JSP in Telangana will likely impact the party's poll prospects in the Andhra Pradesh Assembly elections in the first half of 2024.

Except for Kukatpally in Hyderabad, known to have a significant chunk of voters who have migrated from Andhra Pradesh, the JSP sank. The JSP candidate in Kukatpally, Mummareddy Prem Kumar, finished third behind the Bharat Rashtra Samithi and Congress party candidates, with around a 16 per cent vote share.

Kukatpally is believed to have at least 70,000 Kapu votes, the community to which Pawan Kalyan belongs, and around 40,000 Kamma voters, who are initially from Andhra Pradesh.

In the remaining seven seats that the JSP contested, Khammam, Kothagudem, Wrya, Aswaraopeta, Kodad, Nagarkurnool and Tandur, none of the JSP candidates breached the 5,000-vote mark. Khammam, Kothagudem, and Wyra Assembly segments fall in the border region with Andhra Pradesh.

Manda Krishna 'Madiga'

Manda Krishna is an influential social activist and leader associated with the Madiga Reservation Porata Samiti

(MRPS) in AP and Telangana. Throughout his life, Manda Krishna fought for the rights of Scheduled Caste people, also called Dalits and brought about pride in the downtrodden community. By wearing his Dalit identity with pride, Manda Krishna helped the people of his community rise in self-esteem.
Born in 1965 in the Madiga community, a Scheduled Caste in India, Manda Krishna's journey into activism can be traced back to his formative years when he experienced social inequalities faced by the Madiga community. Determined to address these injustices, he embarked on social reform and activism.

The primary objective of the MRPS, the organisation he started, was to advocate for the rights of the Madiga community and demand proper representation in education, employment, and politics.

One of the central issues Manda Krishna and the MRPS championed is the demand for categorising Scheduled Castes. The Madiga community, like many other Scheduled Castes, faces internal inequalities. Manda Krishna has been at the forefront of the movement to address these disparities by seeking separate reservations within the Scheduled Caste category.

Besides social activism, Manda Krishna contested elections, highlighting issues related to social justice and the rights of marginalised communities. His foray into politics is an extension of his commitment to bringing about systemic change from within the political framework.

Manda Krishna's activism has not been without challenges. His confrontations with the government and other influential groups have been notable. The struggle for categorising Scheduled Castes has faced opposition from various quarters, leading to protests and negotiations.

During the Telangana statehood movement, Manda Krishna and the MRPS played a role in articulating the concerns and aspirations of the Madiga community within the broader context of the demand for a separate state. Manda Krishna's contributions to social justice and activism have earned him recognition and awards. His efforts to highlight and address the challenges faced by the Madiga community have resonated with many, both within and beyond. His legacy is closely tied to his unwavering commitment to social justice and the empowerment of marginalised communities, and he stands as a symbol of resilience and determination in the face of social injustice.

In Telangana, Madigas make up almost 60 per cent of the Scheduled Caste population, constituting about 17 per cent of the total population in the state. The MRPS announced its support to the Bharatiya Janata Party in the Telangana State Assembly elections 2023. This decision, taken under the leadership of Manda Krishna, came after Prime Minister Narendra Modi addressed a public meeting with the MRPS chief and extended his complete support to the longstanding demands of the Madiga community.

In that meeting, Narendra Modi announced that the Union government would soon form a committee that would adopt all possible means to empower the Madigas. Interestingly, since 2013, Narendra Modi has closely interacted with Manda Krishna, and in its 2014 manifesto, the BJP promised internal reservations for Scheduled Castes. However, the Modi government has failed to deliver its promise.

After the public meeting with Modi in November 2023, Manda Krishna called on MRPS cadres as well as members of allied Dalit organisations such as the Mahajana Socialist Party (MSP), Madiga Student Federation (MSF), and others to campaign for the BJP candidates in the Assembly elections. Apart from extending support to the BJP, Manda Krishna accused the Congress party and the BRS of betraying the Madiga community for a long.

The Congress party earlier promised a law allowing for internal reservations, but the party failed to have it ratified by Parliament when it led the Union government. The MRPS leader alleged that the Congress party has done immense injustice to them on the SC sub-categorisation. He accused the Congress party of forgetting all the committee reports favouring the SC sub-categorisation. Following this, Manda Krishna and MRPS cadres campaigned for the BJP. But, the impact has been moderate to low on the electoral fortunes of the saffron party. On the other side, it is widely perceived that the members of the Mala community, another prominent grouping among the SC, are primarily upset with this development and might have gravitated towards the Congress party or the BRS.

Techies in contest

Siddharth Chakravarthy, who sought to contest from Jubilee

Hills, and Akarsh Sriramoju, who joined the race for Serilingampally, were previously employed as IT consultants, leading comfortable lives. However, disillusioned by political corruption and motivated by the absence of educated voices in politics, these young professionals decided to enter the political arena from their respective constituencies. They eschewed high-decibel rhetoric and grand promises, instead focusing on utilising technology and maintaining a straight-forward approach. Both candidates dedicated substantial time to engaging with voters individually, adopting a one-on-one interaction strategy.

Akarsh Sriramoju, with an MSc in cognitive science from the University of Hyderabad and two years of experience in an IT firm, left his job in April 2023 to pursue a political career, aspiring to create a comprehensive transformation in Serilingampally. His primary goal is to raise awareness about constitutional rights and empower constituents to address local issues. In contrast, a tech entrepreneur, Siddharth Chakravarthy, employed advanced technology, such as artificial intelligence through Vako.AI, to connect with voters in Jubilee Hills. Siddharth contended that traditional door-to-door campaigning is outdated, advocating for the use of technology for voter interaction in urban constituencies like Jubilee Hills.

Akarsh identified issues like limited public participation in policy development, inadequate healthcare facilities, unemployment, and deficient infrastructure as crucial concerns in Serilingampally. He formulated his manifesto based on a three-month survey to analyse people's problems, proposing that 40 per cent of MLA Constituency Development

Programme funds annually be allocated to renovate or construct hospitals. Akarsh observed the practical non-existence of medical facilities in each ward. He highlighted the reliance of government schools on NGOs and corporate social responsibility (CSR) funds, receiving minimal support from the government.

Siddharth, an engineering graduate with an MS from the United States who worked in Silicon Valley before returning to India to establish his enterprise, faced initial scepticism from family and friends regarding his decision to run for elections. However, he gained overwhelming support, particularly from his wife, Druthi, a fellow tech entrepreneur. Siddharth's utilisation of artificial intelligence enables voters to engage with him through a scan code, providing access to a WhatsApp chatbox for interaction. Despite facing challenges in capturing voter attention, Siddharth and Akarsh believe that integrating simple technologies and genuine intentions will reshape the electoral landscape, paving the way for more independent candidates in future elections and challenging established political parties.

The Young Turks

The rise of young Turks in politics has been a dynamic and transformative force, injecting fresh perspectives, energy, and innovation into the traditional political landscape. These emerging leaders, often in their 20s and 30s, are challenging the status quo and ushering in a new era of political engagement. Unlike their seasoned counterparts, young Turks are characterised by a willingness to embrace change, leverage technology, and address contemporary issues with a forward-looking approach. Their diversity, in terms of background and ideologies, reflects the changing demographics and evolving aspirations of the electorate.

In many cases, these young leaders have harnessed the power of social media and digital platforms to connect directly with voters, mobilise support, and amplify their messages. Their ability to engage with the youth, who comprise a significant portion of the voting population, has given them a unique advantage in navigating the intricacies of modern politics.

The young Turks often bring a blend of academic acumen, professional experiences, and grassroots activism to the table. Their unconventional thinking and fearlessness in challenging established norms have created a more dynamic and responsive political ecosystem.

While some may view them as disruptors, the emergence of young Turks signals a necessary evolution in political leadership. Their dedication to addressing contemporary challenges, commitment to inclusivity, and emphasis on transparency resonate with a generation seeking a departure from traditional politics. As these rising stars continue to make their mark, they not only redefine the political landscape but also inspire a new generation of leaders who are not afraid to challenge, innovate, and shape the future of governance.

The Telangana Assembly elections 2023 have witnessed some young Turks emerge victorious. They are young, well-educated, and ambitious and made a sensational electoral debut defeating political heavyweights while still in their 20s or 30s.

Here are some of them:

Mamidala Yashaswini Reddy, at the young age of 26, has emerged as a formidable force, achieving a significant upset in the political arena. Contesting on a Congress party ticket from Palakurthi, she secured victory over Erraballi Dayakar Rao, the Minister for Panchayat Raj, who boasts the record of being a six-time MLA and one-time MP.

Notably, Dayakar Rao had never experienced electoral defeat throughout his four-decade-long political career, and his confidence was high as he faced a political novice in Yashaswini. Despite lacking a political background and entering the electoral scene unexpectedly, Yashaswini, with a B.Tech in electronics and communication, pursued her education in Hyderabad before relocating to the United States following her marriage.

Her entry into the contest occurred by chance when her mother-in-law's candidacy faced challenges. In a direct face-off, Yashaswini secured a resounding victory, defeating Dayakar Rao by an impressive margin of over 47,000 votes. This unexpected outcome delivered a significant blow to the 67-year-old Erraballi Dayakar Rao, who had switched from the TDP to TRS (now BRS) in 2016.

In the affidavit submitted during her nomination, Yashaswini revealed her role as an office manager at Raj Properties and Group. Her husband, Rajaram Mohan Reddy, is the finance manager in the same firm, and their combined movable assets amount to Rs 55 crore. In a post-victory interview, Yashaswini acknowledged that becoming an MLA was an unexpected development. However, she was determined to bring about positive changes for those who entrusted her with their votes.

Mynampalli Rohith Rao, a 26-year-old political newcomer, achieved a remarkable debut in the electoral arena by securing victory over the three-time MLA and BRS leader, Padma Devender Reddy, a former deputy Speaker of the Telangana Assembly, in the Medak Constituency.

Rohith, much like Yashaswini, entered the electoral scene with flair and clinched the victory by an impressive margin of over 10,000 votes. Adding to the political narrative, Rohith Rao's father, Mynampalli Hanumanth Rao, was a BRS MLA in the previous Assembly and was again nominated from his Malkajgiri Constituency in Greater Hyderabad. However, discord arose when Hanumanth Rao disagreed with the party's decision to deny his son a ticket from Medak. He insisted Rohith deserved the ticket due to his significant social service in the constituency.

Facing an unyielding stance from KCR, Hanumanth Rao parted ways with the BRS and joined the Congress party under the condition that both he and his son be granted tickets. Although Hanumanth Rao couldn't retain the Malkajgiri seat, he expressed satisfaction that his son commenced his political journey with a triumphant victory.

Rohith Rao, a qualified MBBS professional, doubles as an entrepreneur. He asserts a commitment to positive change through his humanitarian efforts, facilitated by his charitable organisation, 'Mynampally Social Service Organisation.'

Chittam Parnika Reddy, the 30-year-old first-time MLA, hails from a family with a three-generation political legacy. Running as the Congress party candidate, Dr Parnika Reddy, a qualified doctor, won significantly in the Narayanpet Constituency. She emerged triumphant over S. Rajender Reddy, a two-time MLA from the BRS, securing a winning margin of 8,000 votes.

Dr Parnika Reddy completed her MBBS in 2016 and carried the legacy of her late grandfather, former Congress party leader Chittem Narsi Reddy, who tragically lost his life to a Maoist attack in 2005. Her father, C. Venkateswara Reddy, also fell victim to the same attack. Dr Parnika Reddy's aunt, D.K. Aruna, is a BJP vice-president and has served as a former minister.

In the political landscape, Dr Parnika Reddy's uncle, C. Ram Mohan Reddy, a two-time MLA, contested on a BRS ticket from the Makhtal Constituency. However, he faced defeat against the Congress party's Vakiti Srihari with a margin of 17,525 votes. Chittam Parnika Reddy's electoral journey reflects the intertwining threads of family history and political dynamics in her pursuit of public service.

Vedma Bhojju Patel, a youthful leader of the Gond tribe, has become a first-time Member of the Legislative Assembly (MLA) in the Telangana Legislative Assembly. Hailing from Kallurguda in the Utnuru Mandal of the united Adilabad district, Vedma Bhojju is the son of a humble tribal couple, Vedma Bhimrao and Girijabai.

The 37-years-old secured his seat in the Khanapur

Constituency of Nirmal district on a Congress party ticket, triumphing over former BJP MP Ramesh Rathod and NRI Bhukya Jhonson Naik, who ran on a BRS ticket.

Despite his modest background, Vedma Bhojju Patel, who holds an MA and an LLB degree, has a history of active involvement in Adivasi causes. Beginning his journey in the Adivasi Student Association, he later served as a consultant in the Adivasi Rights Struggle Committee (Tudumbama) and worked as a contract employee. Two years ago, Vedma Bhojju decided to resign from his job and join the Congress party, formally aligning himself with the political arena under the guidance of PCC president Revanth Reddy.

Vedma Bhojju Patel, born in poverty, worked as a paper boy in his early years. Even today, he resides in the house allocated to him through the "Indiramma" housing scheme, symbolising a remarkable journey from humble beginnings to legislative success.

His election from Khanapur marks a significant achievement, as he is only the second Gond leader to secure victory in this constituency since the late Kotnak Bheem Rao, a former minister, and that too, after a lapse of three decades. Vedma Bhojju Patel's story is a testament to an ordinary individual's ability to rise to prominence within the Legislative Assembly.

The Gond tribe, one of the largest and oldest tribal communities in India, has a rich cultural heritage that spans centuries. Primarily found in the central and Deccan regions of the country, the Gond people have a distinctive identity shaped by their unique customs, traditions, and art forms.

They are known for their close connection with nature, and their lifestyle revolves around agriculture, hunting, and gathering. The community reveres the natural world deeply, considering it an integral part of their existence. This is reflected in their folklore, rituals, and artistic expressions.

Despite the rich culture, the Gond tribe faces challenges such as socioeconomic disparities, limited access to education, and issues related to land rights.

Revival of Netaji's party

The All-India Forward Bloc (AIFB) emerged as a notable participant in nationwide elections, leaving its mark in various Assembly constituencies in Telugu land. Originating as a left-wing nationalist political entity in India, AIFB took form in 1939 as a breakaway faction from the Congress party under the leadership of Subhas Chandra Bose. Post-independence, it reestablished itself as an independent political party, with West Bengal being its stronghold, currently led by Secretary-General G. Devarajan.

Renowned Indian politicians Sarat Chandra Bose and Chitta Basu played pivotal roles in the party's post-independence journey. In Andhra Pradesh, the party experienced significant influence in the 1950s, though it later declined. Despite a 2005 initiative to revive its Andhra Pradesh State Committee, success eluded AIFB in the region.

In the 2018 Telangana State Assembly elections, AIFB candidate Karukanti Chander defeated the TRS's Somarapu Satyanarayana in the Ramagundam Constituency, with over 45 per cent of the votes. However, Chander later joined the TRS and got a party ticket in 2023. However, he was defeated by the Congress party's Makkan Singh Raj Thakur.

In the 2023 elections, the AIFB once again asserted its presence, influencing outcomes in specific seats. While not securing any victories, it notably impacted the fortunes of other candidates. For instance, in the Kothagudem Constituency, Jalagam Venkat Rao, son of former chief minister Jalagam Vengala Rao, garnered a substantial number of votes, finishing second. In Gadwal, AIFB candidate Gongalla Ranjith Kumar secured a third-place, polling more votes than the BJP and the BSP candidates. Shadnagar saw the AIFB's Palamuru Vishnuvardhan Reddy at third, showcasing significant voter support. In Huzurnagar, AIFB candidate Pillutla Raghu secured a third-place with more votes than the BJP's Challa Srilatha Reddy.

Despite the polarisation between the Congress party and the BRS candidates in Nalgonda, the AIFB's Pilli Rama Raju Yadav finished third, surpassing the BJP's performance in a region with a substantial Muslim voter base. While the popularity of individual candidates may outweigh that of the AIFB in the listed constituencies, the choice of these candidates to contest on the AIFB ticket suggests that its symbol - a "Lion" - resonates with voters in specific areas.

Confusion over symbols

Symbols such as the Truck, Road Roller, and Autorickshaws

became a concern for the ruling Telangana Rashtra Samithi (TRS) in the 2018 Assembly elections. Although a direct link between these symbols and the electoral outcomes of TRS/BRS was not established, an intriguing electoral dilemma surrounding these symbols triggered a heated debate just before the State went to the polls.

Leading up to the 2023 Telangana State Assembly elections, the Election Commission of India drew lots for party symbols, and the "Road Roller" was allotted to the Yuga Tulasi party. This allocation allowed party candidates to contest using the symbol in both Assembly and Lok Sabha elections across the Telugu states of Andhra Pradesh and Telangana. However, Yuga Tulasi party's founder-president, Shiva Kumar, reached a compromise with KCR, opting to contest only in select Assembly constituencies to avoid impacting the prospects of the BRS.

Shiva Kumar explained his decision to the media, "If we don't contest, the symbol will become a free symbol and can be allotted to anyone. In such a case, it can be detrimental to the BRS. Some Congress party and BJP members approached me to allot my symbol to people whose names would match with BRS candidates. There can be confusion with a similar name and symbol, and BRS votes might be polled for the other candidate. I ensured that it did not happen."

Shiva Kumar manages two cow shelters with hundreds of cattle and has been actively rescuing cows in and around Hyderabad from illegal slaughter. He aspires to establish a cow shelter with one lakh cows and to advocate for declaring the cow as the national animal of India. As part of the agreement with the BRS, Shiva Kumar stated that KCR, if elected, promised him land in Ibrahimpatnam to build a cow shelter.

Voting & Verdict

Telangana had 15,871,493 male voters and 15,843,339 female voters, while the number of transgender voters stood at 2,557. The number of voters has increased by 5.8 per cent compared to January 2023. According to the Election Commission reports, 2,202,168 votes were deleted across the State for various reasons.

A total of 2,290 candidates were in the fray, while 608 withdrew their nominations. The most candidates in the electoral contest were from LB Nagar, with 48 candidates, and the least were from Banswada and Narayanpet, each with seven candidates.

Major factors widely debated in the state were:

- Anti-incumbency against BRS after it was in power for 10 years;
- Corruption allegations against the KCR government, which gained momentum after the Medigadda dam developed cracks;
- Opposition's allegations about dynasty-like politics in Telangana;
- Paper leakage from the Telangana State Public Service Commission has hurt the youth;
- Dharani portal, an Integrated Land Records System launched by the BRS government as part of land reforms and to aid farmers in the distribution of the Rythu Bandhu scheme to beneficiaries, has been con-

tested by opposition parties, alleging that it was created to grab the lands of poor farmers.

Strong anti-incumbency generated by the failure to fill government jobs, perceived arrogance of KCR, gaping holes in the coverage of cash transfer schemes, voter fatigue and corruption, land grabbing charges faced by 30 to 40 BRS MLAs, and KCR's "bold" (now widely perceived as ill-conceived) and early decision of fielding most of the BRS MLAs including those with a dubious track record came into play in the poll.

On the day Telangana went to polls, one aspect that was closely monitored was the percentage of voters who would step out and cast their votes according to their preferences. A common trend observed across all elections is that voters living in urban areas do not cast their votes and instead use the day as a holiday to relax or to entertain themselves. However, I always disagreed with this view. Even in urban locations, more than 75 per cent of voters go out to exercise their adult franchise, a democratic right and duty bestowed upon them. However, certain technical anomalies do not capture the actual scenario and depict the turnout low each time. Unfortunately, the Election Commission has not taken any corrective measures to make amends for the discrepancies that have crept in and remain so in the electoral rolls for decades now.

The voting for the Telangana Assembly elections was held on November 30, 2023, and according to the official data made available, the State recorded a voter turnout of 71.34 per cent. The highest polled constituency was Munugode, with

91.89 per cent, while Yakutpura, which ultimately witnessed a see-saw contest between the top two contenders, was the lowest polled at 36.69 per cent.

Among the rural areas, Jangaon has seen a voter turnout of 83.34 per cent, followed by Narsampet (83 per cent), Dubbak (82.75 per cent), Nakrekal (82.34 per cent), Medak (81.72 per cent), Palakurthi (81.23 per cent), Bhongir (81.04 per cent), among others.

On the other hand, the urban areas recorded very low voter turnout. Among the other seats under Hyderabad city limits, Nampally polled 42.76 per cent votes, followed by Charminar (41.45 per cent), Malakpet (41 per cent), Bahadurpura (44.86 per cent), and Chan-drayangutta (45 per cent). All these seats fall under the Old City region of Hyderabad, where the Muslim population is high.

It is widely believed that Muslims vote in large numbers and vote 'en masse' in a certain direction. But the polling percentage numbers throw a different picture. This has been the situation for election after election, but no efforts have been made to address this anomaly.

On the day after Telangana went to the polls, a digital media platform journalist sought my opinion on the low voter turnout in urban areas, specifically in Hyderabad. Her article quoted me: "No, they are voting, but there are dual votes and the old ones are not erased. I would like to give an example. In Hyderabad, a friend has 12 votes registered in their home. Among the 12, only five people are present now, and the rest, being tenants, have moved out. Despite telling the

GHMC officers that they no longer live here, their names are still on the voters' list, and 12 slips were issued. This is a technical error, and they have failed to rectify it despite bringing it to their notice. This is a myth that has been created and is only being amplified. Urban voters are voting, but the additional and dual names are not cleared. If the election commission takes a serious note and carries out an exercise, there will be maximum deletion in urban areas."

Once the Election Commission of India announces the election schedule, non-governmental organisations typically educate people on the importance of democracy and the need to vote. Many NGOs working in this space have reported that all registered voters, or those they helped get registered as voters, have voted. This time in Telangana, many lovers of democracy, like me, expected the voting percentage to increase substantially. But, looking at the final numbers, the rot of wrong electoral rolls is much more deep-rooted.

The population at the individual village level is small, and the sarpanch-led gram panchayat system is more efficient in correcting the electoral rolls than the municipal corporations. The names of young or first-time voters are added, and the names of the deceased or those who shifted out of the villages permanently are deleted on time. Some voters are registered in their respective villages but might work in a city or town. Most of such voters return to their native places to exercise their voting rights. In villages, voting is often a social compulsion, and the welfare benefits they receive are linked to their voting locally.

According to a news report, municipal authorities in cities

might not be as serious in checking the authenticity of the electoral rolls because it is tasked once every five years and going door to door in urban areas is considered a mammoth task. As a combination of all the above reasons, dual votes of people who are missing or not present in the country and even the dead remain in records forever.

The Election Commission announced that a record number of 13,000 cases have been filed concerning the enforcement of the Model Code of Conduct in this election. There has been a marked increase in the postal ballot, with 16,005 seniors aged above 80 and 9,459 persons with disabilities using it, apart from the 1.8 lakh government employees, including the police personnel.

On the polling day, in 13 constituencies impacted by left-wing extremism, polling was wrapped up by 4 pm, and in the remaining ones, it continued up to 5 pm. Those who arrived at the polling station by 5 pm were allowed to exercise their franchise, due to which polling extended up to 9.30 pm. When some rumours started around, Chief Electoral Officer Vikas Raj refuted attributions that the spurt in polling percentage after 5 pm was due to heavy bogus voting. He said the polling had been largely uneventful, except for a few incidents.

The special focus in this election was on setting up polling stations in habitations of "Particularly Vulnerable Tribal Groups", and as a result, seven polling stations had less than 50 voters, and four of them had less than 25 voters. A polling station in the Devarkadra Assembly segment had the lowest number of voters, just eight!

The incumbent Bharat Rashtra Samithi, the Congress party and the Bharatiya Janata Party were the key political parties in the polls, along with the Communist Party of India, the Communist Party of India (Marxist), the Bahujan Samaj Party, the All-India Forward Block, among others. As many as 2,290 candidates, including 221 women and one transgender person, contested the elections.

As per the mandate given by the people of Telangana, the Congress party emerged as the winner, crossing the halfway mark and winning 64 seats in the state. The BRS won 39 seats and will remain the main opposition party in the Legislative Assembly. These were followed by the Bharatiya Janata Party, which won eight, and the All-India Majlis-e-Ittehadul Muslimeen, which won seven. The Congress party ally Communist Party of India won the lone seat of Kothagudem, from which State unit president Kunamneni Sambasiva Rao defeated his rival AIFB candidate with a comfortable margin of 26,547 votes.

Looking at region-wise results, out of the 25 seats in the Greater Hyderabad region, the BRS won 16. It was followed by the AIMIM with seven. The Congress party and the BJP secured one seat each. In North Telangana, out of the total 51 seats, the Congress party bagged 33 seats, while the BRS retained only 10 seats. The most interesting development in this region was the BJP winning seven seats. Out of 43 seats in South Telangana, the Congress party emerged victorious in 30 seats, and BRS candidates won the remaining 13. Such was the decline in the seats for the ruling party that it failed to win even a single seat in 14 out of 33 districts in Telangana. On the other hand, the Congress party swept the region, winning 9 out of 10 seats in the combined Khammam district, 11 out of 12 in the combined Nalgonda district and 12 out of 14 in the combined Mahabubnagar district.

In the North Telangana districts, where the Congress party was considered not so strong, it made considerable inroads, winning 10 out of 12 seats in Warangal, eight out of 12 in Karimnagar, four out of nine in Nizamabad and four out of 10 in Adilabad districts. In the Rangareddy district, the Congress party bagged four seats, while it drew a blank in the seats under the Hyderabad city limits.

A sizeable Muslim wave is believed to have helped the Congress party win many seats, unlike in 2018 when the community backed the BRS candidates. Among the seats that the Congress party won is Warangal West, which it had not won in the last four polls. There are over 60,000 voters from the Muslim community here. Similarly, their vote helped Congress party beat sitting BRS MLAs in Mahbubnagar, Huzurnagar, Warangal East, Khammam, Bodhan, Ibrahimpatnam, Shadnagar, Ramagundam, Nizamabad Rural and Nalgonda. But it was a different story in Greater Hyderabad and surrounding areas, where they backed the BRS and its ally AIMIM. Hyderabad MP Asaduddin Owaisi-led AIMIM retained all its seven seats of Nampally, Charminar, Yakutpura, Chandrayangutta, Karwan, Bahadurpura and Malakpet.

Among the individual candidates, the most prominent win was **Katipally Venkata Ramana Reddy** (KVR) of the Bharatiya Janata Party. He emerged victorious in the

Kamareddy Assembly Constituency, defeating KCR and Revanth Reddy. Though this seat initially attracted attention with two contenders for the Chief Minister post in the fray, it will be remembered forever as the segment that produced a giant killer in the form of KVR.

Kamareddy had 245,822 eligible voters and a significant presence of Scheduled Caste and Scheduled Tribe electors. Ramana Reddy, a businessman-turned-politician, has 11 criminal cases registered against him, including charges relating to rioting, public nuisance and unlawful assembly. Despite a lack of formal education, he is believed to have amassed considerable wealth over the years. According to the affidavit he filed before the Election Commission, KVR's declared assets stood at Rs 49.7 crore, which included Rs 2.2 crore in moveable assets and Rs 47.5 crore as immovable assets.

Ramana Reddy, who dedicated his victory to the people of Kamareddy, began his political journey with the Congress party and was elected as a member of the Mandal Parishad Territorial Council (MPTC) in the erstwhile Nizamabad district during the Y.S. Rajasekhara Reddy government in 2004. He became a Zilla Parishad Territorial Council (ZPTC) member and eventually served as Zilla Parishad chairperson. Following the death of YSR, Ramana Reddy fell out with the local Congress party leadership and tacitly supported the TRS in the 2014 Assembly polls. Later, Ramana Reddy found himself in a controversy after the KCR led TRS accused him of conspiring to murder a party worker. Just ahead of the 2018 Assembly elections, he joined the BJP, which fielded him from the seat and finished a distant third after Gampa

Govardhan of the TRS and Mohammad Shabbir Ali of the Congress party, with a 9.5 per cent vote share.

After the 2018 polls, Ramana Reddy garnered a support base extensively in villages across the constituency and is known to act on people's demands instead of just promising and providing financial aid. Ramana Reddy is believed to have personally oversaw the construction of many community halls across the Kamareddy Constituency.

Ramana Reddy was also at the forefront of the farmers' fight against the Kamareddy town draft master plan, which proposed to acquire about 2,000 acres of land in eight villages adjoining the town for development projects, including an outer ring road and industrial zone. The proposal was met with widespread outrage from villagers earlier this year. Before the election, minister K.T. Rama Rao said that the government had decided to drop the master plan. Farmers of these villages wanted the government to look for barren lands instead of their agricultural lands.

The biggest margin in the Telangana Assembly elections 2023 was registered by **K.P. Vivekananda Goud** of the BRS, who defeated his closest rival, Kuna Srisailam Goud of the BJP, by a whopping margin of 85,576 votes in the Quthbullapur Assembly Constituency. While in the campaign and during a live television debate, Vivekananda Goud had a heated exchange of words with Srisailam Goud and the former grabbed the latter by his throat, a violent reaction that came after the BJP's candidate said, "Your father is an encroacher", to the BRS MLA. The video of the incident went viral on the Internet, evoking sharp criticism from ministers, senior politicians, and people.

Reacting sharply to this incident, Union minister and BJP State unit chief Kishan Reddy wrote on the social media platform "X" (formerly Twitter): "The Hallmark of BRS - Goondaism. A BRS-sitting MLA attacked a BJP MLA candidate from Quthuballapur @KunaSrisailam. It's shocking when a contesting opposition candidate is attacked and scuffled in open public; imagine if the BRS returns to power, even common people will be attacked in the same manner."

Despite this incident, a well-educated and well-mannered Vivekananda Goud won with the highest margin in the state, suggesting his popularity in the constituency. I have known Vivekananda Goud personally since 2014, when he first contested and won as an MLA from Quthbullapur. My friends Nitin Tanksale, Sreekar Reddy and I were involved in Vivekananda's election campaign in 2014.

Thanneeru Harish Rao, former Telangana finance minister and nephew of KCR, is another prominent figure known to have registered enormous victories in the Assembly elections from his Siddipet Constituency. Harish Rao registered his win with 1,05,514 votes and by a margin of 82,308 votes, defeating the Congress party's Pujala Hari Krishna, who secured 20,206 votes and the BJP's Dudi Srikanth Reddy, who secured 23,201 votes.

Harish Rao is among the few candidates who regularly polled over a lakh votes from his constituency. Between 2014 and 2018, Harish Rao served as Telangana's minister for irrigation, marketing and legislative affairs. On September 8

2019, he was appointed as the finance minister during a cabinet expansion, and in November 2021, he was also made the minister for health, medical, and family welfare. Following his victory in 2023, 51-year-old Harish Rao will now be the youngest seven-time member of any Legislative Assembly in India.

My friends Nitin Tanksale, Sreekar Reddy and I were involved in Harish Rao's election campaign in 2014. We ran a highly innovative and first-of-its-kind campaign for Harish Rao. The campaign's concept was based on personalising the content provided by the candidate and creating a one-on-one connection between him and his prospective voters. I must appreciate Harish Rao for understanding the uniqueness and impact of this campaign within five minutes of our pitch to him. Harish Rao had put in a considerable effort to help collate data from across the Siddipet constituency, which would be used for personalised tele-calling with a message from the contestant.

Kale Yadaiah, who won from the Chevella Assembly Constituency, will be remembered for registering a win with the lowest margin in the Telangana Assembly elections in 2023. Kale Yadaiah of the BRS, who polled 76,218 votes, won over Beem Bharath Pamena of the Congress party with a slender margin of just 268 votes. In 2018, Yadaiah secured 99,168 votes in Chevella and won with a comfortable margin of 33,552 votes. Earlier in 2014, Yadaiah, then in the Congress party, won in Chevella with a low margin of just 781 votes.

The Delhi-based Centre for the Study of Developing

Societies (CSDS) conducted a survey as part of its Lokniti programme between November 25 and December 1, 2023. It interviewed 3,097 voters, who were randomly selected, from 120 polling stations in 30 Assembly constituencies for the survey. According to CSDS, a multi-stage systematic random sampling design was adopted to conduct the survey. In each polling station, 40 voters were randomly sampled from the electoral roll, and 25 were interviewed. These interviews were conducted face-to-face at electors' homes by specially trained field investigators, primarily students from various colleges and universities. The questionnaire for the survey was translated into Telugu. Each interview took 15-20 minutes.

The political atmosphere during the Assembly elections was marked by accusations from the Congress party and the BJP against the BRS government. The KCR-led government was accused of corruption throughout its tenure, and the Lokniti-CSDS survey indicated that corruption emerged as a prominent source of dissatisfaction among the voters.

The wealth accumulated by BRS leaders during the party's two terms was quite visible at the village and town levels. Many media reports suggested that the average voter of Telangana was quite shocked and unhappy with how the political class, especially those in power, accumulated wealth. Many alleged that leaders who did not even have a motorcycle started owning expensive four-wheel vehicles.

Close to 50 per cent of the voters in Telangana felt that corruption had increased during the second tenure of the KCR regime, which hurt the BRS's prospects in the elections. However, nearly a quarter of respondents believed that corruption under KCR had decreased, while at least 20 per cent felt there was no change in corruption. Despite the propaganda against the Congress party being a corrupt party, since the UPA-2 government was in power in Delhi, the average Telangana voter seems to think that the Congress party was trying to reduce corruption in this state. As the leader of the statehood agitation, KCR remained popular among those who believe that the creation of Telangana has greatly helped satisfy widespread expectations. Sixty per cent of such voters preferred KCR over the Congress party and the BJP. However, nearly half the voters felt statehood only somewhat addressed people's issues.

Despite the towering image of KCR, his party's extensive grassroots network and welfare programmes, the party failed to emerge victorious because the ruling party had heavily banked on the welfare schemes. However, most of these schemes, except for the Aasara pension, did not reach the people.

The housing scheme, which KCR beautifully packaged and narrated as a "Double Bedroom Scheme", reached the least number of people. This scheme and a few others ended KCR's dream of becoming the first Chief Minister from a south Indian State to score a hat trick win. It is now evident that there is a clear link between people not benefiting from the schemes and a higher vote percentage for the Congress party. The performance of the past government also appears to have motivated voters to turn away from the BRS. Only those voters who were fully satisfied with the government's performance favoured KCR, and even among those who were moderately satisfied with his government's work, 29 per cent wanted to give the Congress party a chance.

The KCR government implemented initiatives and programmes for Scheduled Castes (SC) and Other Backward Classes (OBC). However, a significant majority of SC (82 per cent) and OBC (83 per cent) voters did not reap the benefits of these schemes. This voting pattern indicated a distinct preference for the Congress party, particularly among OBC voters, as 43 per cent of those who did not benefit from the schemes voted for the Congress party.

Though the priority for KCR was higher among Dalits and Adivasis, Revanth Reddy did not trail by far. Who would become the Chief Minister if the Congress party came to power was not an important consideration for voters in this election. Only 14 per cent of voters were influenced by this factor, while 38 per cent made up their voting decision by assessing their respective MLA candidates, where anti-incumbency against the MLA played a big factor.

For 32 per cent of voters, political parties were the most critical consideration, irrespective of who the party would install as the Chief Minister. Given the importance placed on parties, voters sided with the one they perceived to be better. Close to half the voters felt that the BRS was more corrupt than the Congress party, and more than half viewed the BRS as more nepotistic than the Congress party. The selection of Revanth Reddy, who cannot be called a dynast, helped the Congress party in a big way. Above all, many people in Telangana might have decided to give the Congress party, which ensured the birth of the new State after decades of struggle, a chance to run it.

Historically, the Congress party is considered better than other parties for representing marginalised communities. The legacy of leaders like Indira Gandhi, still fondly remembered as "Indiramma", stands advantageous for the party. Schemes introduced and implemented by Dr Y.S. Rajasekhara Reddy also help lift the prospects of the Congress party in Telugu states. Though the BRS was regarded as better concerning Telangana's development, the Congress party stood close behind. Considering these factors, the Congress party appeared to be the better party in the eyes of voters.

Among the female voters, 31 per cent preferred KCR, while Revanth Reddy was close behind, with 26 per cent choosing him. The Congress party leader also built a strong appeal among young voters, which has been visible since he took over the reins as the Telangana Pradesh Congress Committee chief. Among the young voters aged under 25 years, 32 per cent wanted Revanth Reddy as CM, as opposed to 28 per cent who stood with KCR.

Among voters who were 56 years and older, 37 per cent wanted KCR to continue as Chief Minister for another term. While the popular perception is that caste plays a vital role in elections, only 38 per cent of Reddys wanted Revanth Reddy to be the next CM, while 25 per cent still preferred KCR. The success of Rythu Bandhu is seen as the reason for this because a large section of Reddys is landed-class and has been benefitting from the scheme. There was also a perception that if the Congress party or any party other than the BRS came into power, it would restrict the benefits of the Rythu Bandhu scheme to just five acres.

On the other hand, the Bharatiya Janata Party leaders reiterated that the Union government has allocated considerable funds to states, including Telangana, and the schemes being implemented in the State are courtesy of Prime Minister Narendra Modi. But, according to the survey, the State witnessed a lower penetration rate of the schemes introduced by the Modi-led Union government, and on average, three out of five voters did not receive advantages from any of the initiatives the NDA government took. This led to a lack of motivation to vote for the BJP among those who did not benefit. However, there is a strong perception that this scenario might change when India goes to the polls to elect the next prime minister. Narendra Modi will be perceived as the right man for the top job due to his robust approach towards national security and foreign diplomacy.

With the Congress party emerging as the clear winner in the elections and the BRS falling below the 40-seat mark, KCR stepped down from the CM post. While the customary practice is to meet the State governor, Tamilisai Soundararajan, to submit the letter of resignation, KCR instead sent his resignation through an officer on special duty.

Without making any statement, KCR moved out of Hyderabad to his farmhouse, which was spread over 60 acres in Erravalli village under his Gajwel Constituency. Starting in 2014, when he first became Chief Minister of Telangana, KCR took a personal interest in developing Erravalli, Narsannapet, and Chinnamulkanoor villages under Gajwel. I travelled in this region a few times and noticed infrastructure development in these villages. KTR, on the other hand, took to social media platform X, formerly Twitter, to write,

"Grateful to the people of Telangana for giving @BRSparty two consecutive terms of government. Not saddened over the result today, but surely disappointed as it was not in expected line for us. But we will take this in our stride as a learning and will bounce back. Congratulations to the Congress party on winning the mandate. Wishing you Good Luck." KTR addressed a press meet at Telangana Bhavan, and conceded defeat.

Reacting to the results, Prime Minister Narendra Modi posted on X. He wrote, "My dear sisters and brothers of Telangana. Thank you for your support to the @BJP4India. Over the last few years, this support has only been increasing, and this trend will continue in the times to come. Our bond with Telangana is unbreakable, and we will keep working for the people. I also appreciate the industrious efforts of each and every BJP karyakarta".

Political observers are experiencing a sense of déjà vu as the BRS was defeated in the Assembly polls, marking a significant shift in the State a decade after it was formed. Even KCR, who played a vital role in the creation of Telangana in June 2014, couldn't alter the outcome. However, IT employees were grossly disappointed with the result. They took to social media to express their sadness over the election results. KTR, acknowledging the grief among his followers, advised them to "accept things with equanimity."

Two decades ago, a similar fate befell another darling of the IT world, Nara Chandrababu Naidu, in 2004. Naidu, who presented himself as the state's chief executive officer, cultivated relationships with IT experts and business leaders. He showcased the state's IT prowess with the inauguration of HiTech City in 1998 and introduced what he termed a SMART (simple, moral, accountable, responsible, and transparent) government. Naidu enlisted the services of the management consultancy firm McKinsey to craft a Vision 2020 document to make Andhra Pradesh the leading State in terms of the standard of living within a decade through the widespread adoption of Information Technology in development and governance.

However, the tables turned when Congress party leader Dr Y.S. Rajasekhara Reddy, with his charismatic presence, traversed the Andhra Pradesh countryside, establishing a solid connection with rural masses by addressing issues like drought during the peak of summer. Following his padayatra, the Congress party seized power, dismantling the political edifice constructed by "Cyber Babu," the moniker bestowed upon Chandrababu Naidu.

The biggest takeaway for me from the Telangana Assembly elections is that socioeconomic issues play a crucial role in influencing elections, as they are deeply interconnected with the well-being and concerns of the population.

Economic disparities can lead to dissatisfaction among lower-income groups, who may feel marginalised or neglected by the government. Political candidates addressing issues of income inequality may gain support from these demographics. Another critical parameter is rising unemployment and the job security of youth. High unemployment rates or concerns about job security can create anxiety among voters. Candidates who propose effective job creation and economic growth strategies may appeal to those worried about their employment prospects.

Policies related to poverty alleviation and social welfare programs are often key election issues. Candidates who advocate for or against specific welfare measures may attract support or opposition based on voters' views on social and economic assistance. The cost of housing can be a significant concern for many voters. Candidates addressing affordable housing, rent control, or housing market stability issues may resonate with voters facing challenges in this area. The failed promise of providing double-bedroom housing for all eligible families was a significant factor in the defeat of KCR's government. In the future, Revanth Reddy's promise of affordable housing will be put to the test.

Candidates who propose healthcare reforms or advocate for better access to affordable healthcare may also gain support, particularly from voters struggling with medical expenses. The availability and quality of education are critical socioeconomic issues. Candidates focusing on education reform and improving access to quality education appeal to voters prioritising these concerns. In their manifesto, the Congress party made tall promises on education, like building international schools at the mandal level. Only time will decide if Revanth Reddy's government fulfilled this promise to the people's satisfaction.

The economic disparities between rural and urban areas can impact electoral outcomes, and candidates addressing the unique challenges faced by each demographic may gain support based on the specific concerns of these communities.

Economic indicators like inflation and the overall cost of living can directly impact voters' daily lives. The Telangana elections exposed how parties fared in convincing the voters on these parameters.

Present & Future

"Cometh the hour, cometh the man."

When the situation is tough, and when the time comes, a man who can turn the tide, and win the situation comes

On December 3, 2023, when history was getting scripted and the Congress party surged ahead of the then-incumbent Bharat Rashtra Samithi, the Gandhi Bhavan came to life after nearly 15 years. There was a sense of triumph among the party leaders and cadres. Many leaders from across all districts of Telangana thronged at Revanth Reddy's residence in Jubilee Hills, Hyderabad.

The man of the moment, Revanth Reddy, who everyone was convinced would become the next Chief Minister of Telangana State, would have been a relaxed man after months and years of turmoil and struggle. After starting his day by a meeting with Anjani Kumar, Director General of Police. Sanjay Jain, a nodal officer with the Telangana State Police, and Mahesh Bhagwat, a nodal officer for expenditure with the State police, also met Revanth Reddy.

The Election Commission of India immediately suspended Anjani Kumar for violating the model code of conduct and observed that the action of DGP could have influenced junior officers in the State police as he met Revanth Reddy even before the final results were declared. On the direction of the Election Commission, Telangana chief secretary A Santhi Kumari issued orders stating that Ravi Gupta, a senior police

officer, is placed in the additional charge of the DGP post. Even as these senior police officers bungled with their administrative responsibilities, Revanth Reddy embarked on a roadshow from his residence to Gandhi Bhavan, the Congress party headquarters in the city. Thousands joined the roadshow to greet the man of the moment, who emerged as the man of the masses. Revanth Reddy dedicated the victory of the Congress party to the martyrs who laid their lives for the cause of Telangana.
Addressing the large gathering of party workers and fans, Revanth Reddy "assured the revival of democracy Telangana" and said that the Pragathi Bhavan, where KCR resided for almost a decade, and the Secretariat buildings will be opened for people to visit to express their grievances.

Though it was destined, the Congress party's formal announcement of Revanth Reddy as the Chief Minister of Telangana came 48 hours after the electoral victory. Congress general secretary K.C. Venugopal, on December 5, 2023, announced Revanth Reddy as the Telangana CM in Delhi after a series of discussions held by the party's central leadership amidst competing claims for the top post.

Before this formal announcement, the Congress Legislative Party passed a unanimous resolution to authorise AICC president Mallikarjun Kharge to appoint a CLP leader who would become the Chief Minister. Revanth Reddy, the State Congress party chief, moved the resolution. It was seconded by Mallu Bhatti Vikramarka, N. Uttam Kumar Reddy, Damodar Raja Narasimha, Komatireddy Venkat Reddy, Sridhar Babu, Ponam Prabhakar, Tummala Nageshwara Rao, D. Anasuya and Prem Sagar.

Oath Ceremony & Sonia Gandhi

Since 1983, when the then Chief Minister-elect, Nandamuri Taraka Rama Rao, took his inaugural oath amid grandeur at the LB Stadium, this venue became a preferred choice for popular chief ministers aiming to make significant political statements. While Marri Chenna Reddy chose the Nizam College Grounds, Dr Y.S. Rajashekhara Reddy preferred Lal Bahabur Stadium in Hyderabad. So did Revanth Reddy now. This event was called the swearing-in ceremony for "Praja Prabutvam", or the people's government. Elaborate preparations were made under the watchful eye of DGP Ravi Gupta, with a security force of 1,500 police personnel.

In every election cycle for the Telangana state since 2014, the leaders of the Congress party consistently proclaimed their victory, pledging to dedicate it as a tribute to Sonia Gandhi for her decisive role in the bifurcation of united Andhra Pradesh. Despite these claims, the Congress party faced electoral setbacks in 2014 and again in 2018, failing to secure a win in Telangana. Ever since assuming the role of the Telangana Pradesh Congress Committee chief, Revanth Reddy echoed similar sentiments, promising that a victory in Telangana would be a special gift to Sonia Gandhi. Revanth Reddy organised a grand celebration when this prophecy was finally fulfilled, presenting the triumph as a gift to Sonia Gandhi.

The creation of Telangana state in 2014 unfolded against a backdrop of tension within the then-ruling Congress party. Sonia Gandhi is widely believed to have played a pivotal role in driving the bifurcation Bill that ultimately resulted in the emergence of India's youngest state. Sonia Gandhi reached out to Venkaiah Naidu of the BJP to ensure the Bill's smooth passage through Parliament. In a decisive action, she expelled six MPs of the Congress party, who had issued a notice for a no-confidence motion against the Manmohan Singh government. This strategic move was aimed to prevent any disruptions in Parliament that could jeopardise the Bill's approval.

The Telangana unit of the Congress party has consistently asserted its role in the state's formation, proudly attributing it to Sonia Gandhi. They have been continuously reminding Telangana voters that her sacrifices were instrumental in realising the dreams and aspirations of the region's people. In 2020, State Congress party leaders even advocated for including a dedicated chapter in school syllabi, highlighting Sonia Gandhi's significant contributions to the formation of Telangana.

On December 7, 2023, Revanth Reddy marked his oath-taking ceremony distinctively, arriving in an open-top jeep and acknowledging the cheers of an enthusiastic crowd of at least 30,000 people at the stadium. Accompanying him was "Sonia amma." Despite being the event's focal point, Revanth Reddy deliberately maintained a low-key understated presence. His choice of wearing a simple white shirt and black trouser added no noteworthy flair to his attire. Instead, he allowed Sonia Gandhi to take centre stage as the vehicle, carrying both of them, leisurely traversed through the passageway and reached the dais.

Revanth Reddy, perceived as an outsider, achieved the position of the State unit chief within six years of joining the Congress party, attributing his ascent to Sonia Gandhi. By presenting the former president of the Congress party to the people of Telangana and standing beside her, Revanth Reddy conveyed a powerful message to both his supporters and critics.

He successfully projected that he enjoyed the support and blessings of the Gandhi family, a factor he believed would solidify his position in the state. Also present at this swearing-in were AICC president Mallikarjun Kharge, Karnataka Chief Minister Siddaramaiah, Himachal Pradesh Chief Minister Sukhvinder Singh Sukhu, Rahul Gandhi, Priyanka Gandhi, and other senior Congress party leaders.

Revanth Reddy was administered the oath of office and the oath of secrecy by Governor Tamilisai Soundararajan. Inducted into the cabinet as the Deputy Chief Minister was Bhatti Vikramarka Mallu. The following individuals, in the specified order, were then administered the oath of office and secrecy as ministers in Revanth Reddy's cabinet: Uttam Kumar Reddy, Damodar Raja Narasimha, Komatireddy Venkat Reddy, Duddilla Sridhar Babu, Ponguleti Srinivasa Reddy, Ponnam Prabhakar, Konda Surekha, Danasari Anasuya (Seethakka), Tummala Nageswara Rao, and Jupally Krishna Rao.

Forecasting public mood is challenging, and the political landscape can undergo significant transformations during election seasons. The Bharat Jodo Yatra led by Congress party leader Rahul Gandhi emerged as one of the numerous factors in Telangana, altering the electoral dynamics. Beyond political figures, various civil society groups and community organisations played pivotal roles in securing the Congress party's victory, evidenced by the voting patterns highlighted by the CSDS study. In the pre-election period, observations indicated a desire among voters in Telangana to oppose the perceived "feudal" tendencies of the then-ruling Bharat Rashtra Samithi.

The BRS leader and former Chief Minister KCR's construction of barricades around his camp office, symbolising a feudal order, drew public scrutiny. The substantial expenditure of nearly Rs 50 crore on these barricades, as revealed in an RTI reply, exemplified KCR's governing style. The Congress party's "Praja Vani" emerged as a response to counteract such practices.

The newly-elected Chief Minister, Revanth Reddy, dismantled these barricades, symbolising a shift towards a more open and inclusive approach. Initiatives like the Mahalaxmi scheme, providing free bus rides for women and transgender individuals, and the Arogyasri scheme, ensuring financial protection for the health needs of underprivileged populations, have contributed to the populace's contentment with the new government.

However, the Congress party must be mindful of the fleeting nature of the honeymoon period. As the party's manifesto outlined, the electorate's mandate calls for more inclusive governance. Issues such as fee hikes at Osmania University, delayed exams, and sluggish recruitment in the higher education sector demand attention. The Congress party, having won many seats reserved for Schedule Castes and Schedule

Tribes, is responsible for fulfilling the promises articulated in its manifesto.

The division of Andhra Pradesh raised questions for numerous communities, especially those categorised as backward castes. A caste census could shed light on the socioeconomic mobility of various communities, aiding in the pursuit of social justice. The Congress party must carefully navigate communal dynamics, particularly considering the BJP's increased vote share in Telangana. The appointment of the AIMIM's Akbaruddin Owaisi as a pro-tem speaker was strategic, but broader community representation remains crucial.

Challenges surrounding schemes like Dharani, Rythu Bandhu, and free power promise necessitate meticulous scrutiny and adjustments to enhance their people-centric nature. The composition of the Revanth Reddy Cabinet, representing diverse social groups, should avoid the perception of being dominated by a single community. Similar to the Congress party government in Karnataka, a balanced development paradigm, combining welfare initiatives with growth, is essential for holistic progress in Telangana. Collaborations with civil society and community-based organisations can play a pivotal role in shaping such a development model.

CM swings into action

Immediately after being sworn in, Chief Minister Revanth Reddy swung into action and signed a file to implement the Six Guarantees as promised by the Congress party in its election manifesto and widely propagated during the election campaign. Rajini, a young woman from Nampally with special needs, was promised a job by Revanth Reddy during the campaign, and the latter signed on a second file, which was an appointment letter for Rajini. A post-graduate in education, Rajini reached out to Revanth Reddy seeking employment as she was having trouble finding a job in the private sector.

Addressing the large gathering, Revanth Reddy said, "Indiramma Rajyam, under his stewardship, will fulfil the aspirations of four crore Telangana people, especially farmers, students, unemployed youth, activists and families of martyrs. Democracy has been decimated in Telangana for the last 10 years, and human rights were violated. People were living in silence as they did not have a platform to bring their grievances to the notice of the previous government." The "Praja Telangana government" was formed with the support of four crore people and the Congress party activists who carried the party flag during the difficult times and elections.

In a bold declaration during his swearing-in ceremony, Revanth Reddy proclaimed that the barriers surrounding Pragathi Bhavan had been dismantled, inviting everyone to enter and share their thoughts and aspirations. The images of workers dismantling the iron barricades with gas cutters and bulldozers symbolised the change in Telangana.

Renaming Pragati Bhavan as Jyotiba Phule Praja Bhavan, Revanth Reddy also announced the initiation of Praja Darbars to address public grievances. This initiative promptly commenced on December 8, 2023. Taking a solemn pledge, Revanth Reddy asserted, "I am committed to protecting the rights of the people, ensuring peace and security for the city's development, competing globally in the progress of Telangana, and instilling confidence in the marginalised that they are not neglected."

Expressing gratitude for the opportunity bestowed upon him by the people, he emphasised his responsibility to serve and not rule. "With inspiration drawn from Sonia Gandhi and Mallikarjuna Kharge and under the guidance of Rahul Gandhi, the new government, named "Indiramma Rajyam," is poised to deliver services with a servant's mentality for the state's development. I consider it a profound honour that the people have entrusted me with the opportunity to contribute to the progress of this region," the new Chief Minister declared.

On December 8, 2023, hundreds lined up outside the Jyotiba Phule Praja Bhavan, formerly Pragathi Bhavan, to attend the Praja Darbar by Revanth Reddy. As announced after taking the oath, Revanth Reddy arrived to meet the people at 10 am, and with the barricades around the Praja Bhavan removed, the gates to the sprawling complex were opened for the first time in nearly 10 years for people to meet the Chief Minister. Revanth Reddy promised to hold the Praja Darbar every week so that citizens could approach him directly with their grievances.

The 'New' Assembly

On December 9, 2023, the first session of the third Telangana State Legislative Assembly began with the oath-taking process of the newly-elected MLAs. Chief Minister

Revanth Reddy was the first to take the oath, followed by Deputy Chief Minister Mallu Bhatti Vikramarka. Sixth-time MLA Akbaruddin Owaisi of the AIMIM presided over the proceedings as the pro-tem Speaker, a responsibility he held until a new Speaker was elected in the House.

The Congress party government dedicated two of the Six Guarantees to people in Telangana on December 9, 2023, which also happens to be the birthday of Sonia Gandhi. The Congress party government extended Rs 10 lakh worth of medical and health services under the Rajiv Arogyasri scheme as part of the two guarantees. The second guarantee was the Mahalaxmi scheme, which allowed all women in Telangana State to travel on the RTC bus services free of cost. The Chief Minister further explained that the Six Guarantees given by the Congress party during the polls were formulated keeping in mind the poor and marginalised sections of the society, and all six guarantees will be implemented within the first 100 days of his administration.

Infrastructure overhaul

In his first week as the Chief Minister, Revanth Reddy outlined his vision, announced vital decisions, and made insightful observations that signal a paradigm shift in the infrastructure development of Telangana, particularly in Hyderabad. Emphasising a comprehensive approach, he underscored the need for balanced development and expansion within the city. He envisioned Hyderabad as a global city with limitless potential, free from geographical constraints. Recognising the fact that 40 per cent of Telangana is urban, Revanth Reddy proposed a strategic plan for

Hyderabad's growth. He advocated for the development of satellite townships encircling the Outer Ring Road (ORR), initially envisioning the city's capacity to accommodate around two crore residents and eventually reaching a population of three crores. The Metro Rail system would be pivotal in this vision, ensuring affordable and rapid connectivity to these satellite townships.

Revanth Reddy has directed senior officers to temporarily halt the current Metro Rail alignment plan to Rajiv Gandhi International Airport and its tender process. Instead, he urged the swift preparation of alternative alignments connecting Mahatma Gandhi Bus Station to Falaknuma and from LB Nagar, passing through Chandrayangutta to the airport.

Hyderabad Metro Rail Limited's managing director was explicitly tasked with devising cost-effective alternatives for extending the Metro line. This includes evaluating two potential routes: one via Mailardevpally, Jalpally, and P7 Road, and another via Barkas to Pahadishareef and Srisailam Road. He emphasised that if a straight-line alignment could reduce costs, it should traverse open areas within the Airport premises, given that the land is government-owned.

The Chief Minister also advised senior officers to plan an environmentally friendly mega township on the expansive lands acquired for Pharma City near Kandukur. Expressing concern about potential pollution, he recommended locating Pharma City at a distance from Hyderabad. Furthermore, he instructed the managing director of HMRL to strategise Metro Rail connectivity to this proposed mega township from the Airport area via Tukkuguda on Srisailam Road.

Expressing dissatisfaction with the allocation of benefits to the metro rail concessionaire L&T MRHL despite the incomplete 5.5 km stretch in the Old City, the Chief Minister instructed senior officers to investigate the matter thoroughly. Emphasising the need to safeguard the government's interests, he called for a comprehensive examination of the concession agreement for L&T MRHL, GMR Airport, and the supplementary concession agreement of metro rail.

Highlighting his government's commitment to a balanced approach between welfare schemes and city development, Revanth Reddy directed senior officers to formulate a master plan for the city. This plan, according to him, should encompass the beautification of the Musi River and leverage the available right of way along its banks to design an east-west road-cum-Metro Rail connectivity from Nagole to Gandipet, linking seamlessly with the intercity bus terminal of MGBS. Encouraging officials to think ambitiously, he urged them to tap into Hyderabad's potential as a logistics and medical hub connecting Western and Gulf countries and South East Asia. Additionally, he instructed the planning of a dry port, considering Telangana's landlocked status.

Revanth Reddy instructed officials to identify parcels of land spanning 500 to 1,000 acres between the Outer Ring Road and the proposed Regional Ring Road to establish industrial zones. These new zones should be strategically located within 50 to 100 kilometres from the airport, national highways, and State highways. He stressed on the importance of acquiring only uncultivable land to mitigate any harm to farmers, aiming to decentralise developmental projects and reduce pollution.

In his directive, Revanth Reddy requested details from officials regarding allocated land for industries and information on parcels that remain unused for industrial purposes. Emphasising on non-polluting industries, he instructed officials to explore alternatives to existing industrial areas such as Nacharam, Jeedimetla, and Katedan in Hyderabad. Additionally, he urged officials to study the policies implemented by Middle Eastern and European countries concerning the establishment of bulk drug factories.

He underscored the need for upcoming industries to be situated away from residential areas, a measure aimed at acquiring lands at more affordable prices with the support of local farmers. He also directed officials to take steps to ensure that industries utilise solar power instead of thermal power and called for the formulation of plans to develop villages as model villages in the state. Seeking information on the status of IDPL land in the Balanagar industrial area, the Chief Minister requested a comprehensive report.

The "Human Face"

Revanth Reddy recommended implementing measures to minimise inconvenience to the general public during the Chief Minister's convoy movement on busy roads.

The CM convoy was streamlined and reduced from 15 vehicles, used during the KCR government, to just nine vehicles. Emphasising the importance of personal field visits to understand the challenges faced by the public, the Chief Minister advised police officials to explore alternative strategies to prevent traffic disruptions and avoid halting vehicular traffic along his travel routes. Revanth Reddy expressed his commitment to addressing people's issues, highlighting the necessity of finding solutions that ensure a smooth experience for the public during his road travels.

Telangana Bhavan in Delhi

The government of Telangana is considering the construction of a new Telangana Bhavan in New Delhi to reflect the rich cultural heritage of Telangana. Revanth Reddy has placed a special emphasis on the equitable division of assets between Telangana and Andhra Pradesh, particularly concerning the existing Telangana and Andhra Pradesh Bhavans in Delhi.

The Chief Minister conducted a comprehensive review of the matter in a meeting with Telangana Bhavan Resident Commissioner Gaurav Uppal and OSD Sanjay Jaju. He sought details regarding the total area of the building, its current condition, and Telangana's allocated space within the Bhavan.

According to the information provided by officials, the undivided land spans 19.78 acres. This includes the Sabari Block, internal roads, and Godavari Block covering 8.781

acres, the Old Nursing Hostel on 3.359 acres, and Pataudi House on 7.641 acres. When inquiring about Telangana's share, officials clarified that Telangana would receive 8.245 acres, while Andhra Pradesh's share would be 11.536 acres under the AP State Reorganisation Act. The Act mandates a division of assets in the ratio of 41.68:58.32 between Telangana and AP.

He also expressed concern about the current condition of the buildings, including the residences of officers and staff, as many structures were built several decades ago. Resident Commissioner Gaurav Uppal informed Revanth Reddy that a significant number of buildings are in a dilapidated state, with ongoing repair work. He emphasised the need for a new building that truly represents the cultural traditions of Telangana.

Tussle in the Assembly

The Telangana State Legislative Assembly has not witnessed substantial debates since its establishment in 2014. The proceedings have been predominantly influenced by the ruling TRS (which became BRS later), led by KCR, resulting in a lack of vigorous discussions. The Chief Minister and his adept ministers, including Harish Rao, KTR, Etela Rajender, and Niranjan Reddy (who joined the Cabinet in the second term), have consistently presented compelling arguments, overshadowing the weak Opposition.

During this period, the Opposition struggled to field leaders who could effectively challenge the government with thorough preparation and a profound understanding of various legislative subjects. However, with Revanth Reddy assuming office as the second Chief Minister of Telangana, there has been a notable shift. He is supported by a team of experienced ministers who previously served in the cabinets of united Andhra Pradesh.

Despite the formidable challenge being faced by the BRS in its role as the main opposition party, leaders like Harish Rao and KTR continue to dominate the opposition front. While other BRS members may also contribute to these discussions, their effectiveness remains untested.

Within two weeks of assuming power, the ruling Congress party strategically cornered the Bharat Rashtra Samithi by releasing "White Papers" on the State of the Telangana economy. The Revanth Reddy government adopted a commendable approach, initiating debates on the floor of the Legislative Assembly. By presenting white papers, the Congress party government compelled the main opposition, which had been in power for almost a decade or two terms, to defend its past decisions. Given this unexpected turn of events, members of the opposition benches find it challenging to source records or information effectively.

What is a White Paper?

A white paper released by a government on the financial health of a State is typically a detailed and comprehensive document that provides an in-depth analysis of the state's economic and financial situation. These papers are often published by government agencies, such as the finance ministry or a State treasury department, and they communicate important information to the public, policymakers, and other stakeholders.

White Paper on the financial health

Economic Overview: An assessment of the state's overall economic performance, including GDP growth, employment rates, inflation, and other relevant economic indicators.

Revenue and Expenditure Analysis: A breakdown of the state's revenue sources, including taxes, grants, and other income, and an analysis of government expenditures across various sectors such as education, healthcare, infrastructure, and public services.

Debt and Liabilities: Information on the state's debt levels, including details on outstanding loans, bonds, and other financial liabilities. This section may also discuss the state's debt management strategy.

Budgetary Policies: An overview of the state's budgetary policies and fiscal strategies. This could include information on how the government plans to raise revenue, allocate resources, and manage fiscal deficits.

Financial Risks and Challenges: Identifying and discussing potential financial risks and challenges the State may face, such as economic downturns, changes in federal funding, or other external factors.

Future Projections: Forecasts and projections for key economic and financial indicators, providing insights into the state's anticipated financial trajectory in the coming years.
Policy Recommendations: In some cases, white papers may include policy recommendations or proposed initiatives to address financial challenges and improve the state's overall economic health.

These white papers are valuable tools for transparency and accountability, helping citizens, investors, and policymakers make informed decisions based on a clear understanding of the state's financial condition. They are usually released periodically, such as annually or biennially, to provide updated information and analysis.

White Paper on the state's finances

"Telangana has experienced a ten-fold increase in its total

outstanding debt since 2014, soaring from Rs 72,658 crore at the state's inception to Rs 6.71 lakh crore under the BRS government's administration until November 2023. The debt composition in 2014, primarily stemming from Budget borrowing for the fiscal year 2014-15, surged to Rs 6,71,757 crore in FY 2023-24. Of this amount, Budget borrowing within FRBM limits accounted for Rs 3,89,673 crore, government-guaranteed loans raised by SPVs and serviced by the government amounted to Rs 1,27,208 crore, government-guaranteed loans raised and serviced by SPVs totalled Rs 95,462 crore, and non-guaranteed loans raised and serviced by SPVs, corporations, or institutions stood at Rs 59,414 crore. The debt service burden escalated from Rs 6,954 crore in 2014-15 to Rs 32,939 crore in 2023-24, representing a substantial annual growth rate of 22 per cent. Despite this substantial debt, the BRS regime has failed to create tangible fiscal assets corresponding to the funds expended over the past decade. The financial strain has become so severe that the government now relies on loans even for day-to-day expenses."

"The actual expenditure figures exhibit an upward trajectory, increasing from Rs 62,306 crore in FY 2014-15 to Rs 2,04,085 crore in FY 2022-23. However, the percentage share of actual expenditure in the overall budget estimates raises concerns. Despite the lowest level of actual expenditure as a percentage of budget estimates (61.9 per cent) in FY 2014-15, the state, on average, spent only 82.3 per cent of the budgeted expenditure between 2014 and 2023. In FY 2021-22, Telangana had one of the highest gaps between budgeted and actual expenditure among General States, with only Punjab having a lower proportion of actual expenditure to budget estimates.

The budgetary process appears flawed and over-optimistic, with inflated receipts and boosted expenditures leading to payment delays and commitments spill-over."

"The Telangana government's inability to achieve budgeted expenditure is attributed to a shortfall in collections compared to budgeted revenue receipts. The need for rationalising budget forecasting mechanisms is emphasised, calling for realistic budgeting practices to narrow the gap between budgeted expenditures and actuals. The C&AG has consistently raised these concerns in their audit reports submitted to the State Legislature."

"In the period from FY 1956-57 to FY 2013-14, before the bifurcation of Andhra Pradesh, Telangana witnessed a significant increase in its share of the combined state's expenditure, growing from Rs 33 crores to Rs 56,947 crores over 57 years. Notably, this period saw substantial development with crucial assets, including infrastructure projects, irrigation projects, drinking water initiatives, universities, medical colleges, hospitals, and extensive infrastructure developments. The establishment of major defence organisations and public sector undertakings, along with the emergence of Hyderabad as a significant defence and research hub, contributed to the state's growth."

"However, since the formation of Telangana in 2014, there has been a stark contrast in its financial trajectory. The outstanding debt, which stood at Rs 72,658 crores in FY 2014-15, has surged to Rs 3,89,673 crores by FY 2022-23, and the debt-to-GSDP ratio has almost doubled in eight years, reaching 27.8 per cent in FY 2023-24. The state's revenue receipts have shown volatility, and the debt-servicing burden has grown significantly, consuming more revenues."

"The debt composition includes government-guaranteed loans raised by SPVs and serviced by the government, government-guaranteed loans raised and serviced by SPVs, and non-guaranteed loans raised and serviced by SPVs, corporations, or institutions. Despite being legally and technically not on the state's books, the debt serviced by the government in the first category is considered part of the state's total debt burden. The debt-servicing burden from off-budget borrowings has risen substantially, contributing to 34 per cent of the total debt-servicing burden in FY 2023-24."

"There is also concern about the higher interest rates ranging from 8.93 per cent to 10.49 per cent incurred by the top five corporations/entities, accounting for 95 per cent of outstanding government guarantees, compared to the average interest rate of 7.63 per cent for Open Market Borrowings. The government, effectively bearing the higher interest burden, is further constrained in its financial situation."

"In conclusion, Telangana faces a challenging fiscal scenario marked by a significant surge in debt, escalating debt-servicing burden, and concerns over budgetary processes. Addressing these issues requires a comprehensive approach, including realistic budgeting practices, expenditure control, and strategic financial management."

Crisis over power supply?

The previous administration led by KCR in Telangana made

a significant commitment to provide continuous and high-quality power to households, agriculture, and industries around the clock. Undoubtedly, since the inception of the new state, people in both urban and rural areas have experienced improved and mostly uninterrupted power supply. Regardless of criticisms against the BRS government, it diligently ensured the procurement and distribution of power to all segments of society.

In contrast, the Congress party government under Revanth Reddy disputed the bold claims made by its predecessor, asserting that the earlier government only provided farmers with 12-14 hours of power. Revanth Reddy announced an intention to launch a judicial inquiry into the power purchase agreements with Chhattisgarh and the previous BRS government's construction of the Bhadradri and Yadadri thermal power plants.

According to a white paper on the energy sector, Telangana's power distribution companies are burdened with a debt of Rs 81,516 crore, with accumulated losses amounting to Rs 62,461 crore. Of this debt, Rs 30,406 crore was borrowed as working capital primarily for settling power charges to generators. Despite this, discoms still owe Rs 28,673 crore in generation and transmission dues as of December 2023. The financial strain on discoms is exacerbated by the government's failure to pay power bills, with a total outstanding of Rs 28,842 crore, including Rs 14,193 crore from lift irrigation projects. The government's default in paying committed true-up charges of Rs 14,928 crore has further contributed to the worsening financial situation of discoms.

At the time of State formation, TS GENCO's installed generation capacity was 4365.26 megawatts. Before statehood, projects with a capacity of 2,960 MW were initiated. Special provisions in the AP Reorganisation Act 2014 allowed the State to receive over 1,800 MW of power beyond the installed capacity. Post-state formation, only one power project of 1,080 MW capacity was commissioned at Bhadradri Thermal Power Stations (BTPS), which is facing significant delays and cost overruns using subcritical technology. Another power project of 4,000 MW in Nalgonda District (Yadadri Thermal Power Station) incurred avoidable coal transport costs of over Rs 800 crore an annum due to its distant location from coal mines, costs that are expected to rise over the project's entire lifespan.

CONSTITUENCY-WISE RESULTS

Constituency Name	Winner				Runner Up				Margin
	Candidate	Party	Votes	%	Candidate	Party	Votes	%	
Sirpur	Palvai Harish Babu	BJP	63,702	34.09	Koneru Konappa	BRS	60,614	32.43	3,088
Chennur (SC)	Gaddam Vivekanand	INC	87,541	57.51	Balka Suman	BRS	50,026	32.86	37,515
Bellampalli (SC)	Gaddam Vinod	INC	82,217	57.96	Durgam Chinnaiah	BRS	45,339	31.96	36,878
Mancherial	Kokkirala Premsagar Rao	INC	1,05,945	55.03	Verabelli Raghunath	BJP	39,829	20.69	66,116
Asifabad (ST)	Kova Laxmi	BRS	83,036	44.97	Ajmera Shyam	INC	60,238	32.62	22,798
Khanapur (ST)	Vedma Bhojju	INC	58,870	33.79	Johnson Naik Bhukya	BRS	54,168	31.09	4,702
Adilabad	Payal Shanker	BJP	67,608	35.84	Jogu Ramanna	BRS	60,916	32.29	6,692
Boath (ST)	Anil Jadhav	BRS	76,792	44.13	Soyam Bapu Rao	BJP	53,992	31.03	22,800
Nirmal	Alleti Maheshwar Reddy	BJP	1,06,400	54.03	Allola Indrakaran Reddy	BRS	55,697	28.28	50,703
Mudhole	Rama Rao Pawar	BJP	98,252	48.59	Gaddigari Vittal Reddy	BRS	74,254	36.72	23,999
Armur	Paidi Rakesh Reddy	BJP	72,658	44.9	Prodduturi Vinay Kumar Reddy	INC	42,989	26.56	29,669
Bodhan	P. Sudarshan Reddy	INC	66,963	38.95	Mohammed Shakil Aamir	BRS	63,901	37.17	3,062
Jukkal (SC)	Laxmi Kantha Rao Thota	INC	64,489	39.19	Hanmant Shinde	BRS	63,337	38.49	1,152
Banswada	Pocharam Srinivas Reddy	BRS	76,278	47.65	Eanugu Ravinder Reddy	INC	52,814	32.99	23,464
Yellareddy	K. Madan Mohan Rao	INC	86,989	47.07	Jajala Surendar	BRS	62,988	34.08	24,001
Kamareddy	Katipally Venkata Ramana Reddy	BJP	66,652	34.55	Kalvakuntla Chandrashekar Rao	BRS	59,911	31.06	6,741
Nizamabad Urban	Dhanpal Suryanarayana Gupta	BJP	75,240	40.82	Mohammed Ali Shabbir	INC	59,853	32.47	15,387
Nizamabad Rural	Rekulapally Bhoopathi Reddy	INC	78,378	40.19	Bajireddy Goverdhan	BRS	56,415	28.93	21,963

Constituency Name	Winner				Runner Up				Margin
	Candidate	Party	Votes	%	Candidate	Party	Votes	%	
Balkonda	Vemula Prashanth Reddy	BRS	70,417	40.28	Muthyala Sunil Kumar	INC	65,884	37.68	4,533
Korutla	Kalvakuntla Sanjay	BRS	72,115	39.28	Dharmapuri Arvind	BJP	61,810	33.67	10,305
Jagtial	M. Sanjay Kumar	BRS	70,243	39.83	T. Jeevan Reddy	INC	54,421	30.86	15,822
Dharmapuri (SC)	Adluri Laxman Kumar	INC	91,393	50.3	Koppula Eshwar	BRS	69,354	38.17	22,039
Ramagundam	Makkan Singh Raj Thakur	INC	92,227	60.28	Korukanti Chandar Patel	BRS	35,433	23.16	56,794
Manthani	Duddilla Sridhar Babu	INC	1,03,822	52.82	Putta Madhukar	BRS	72,442	36.86	31,380
Peddapalli	Chinthakunta Vijaya Ramana Rao	INC	1,18,888	57.17	Dasari Manohar Reddy	BRS	63,780	30.67	55,108
Karimnagar	Gangula Kamalakar	BRS	92,179	40.12	Bandi Sanjay Kumar	BJP	89,016	38.74	3,163
Choppadandi (SC)	Medipally Satyam	INC	90,395	49.62	Sunke Ravishankar	BRS	52,956	29.07	37,439
Vemulawada	Aadi Srinivas	INC	71,451	41.03	Chalimeda Lakshmi Narasimha Rao	BRS	56,870	32.66	14,581
Sircilla	K. T. Rama Rao	BRS	89,244	47.28	K. K. Mahender Reddy	INC	59,557	31.56	29,687
Manakondur (SC)	Kavvampally Satyanarayana	INC	96,773	52.08	Erupula Balakishan	BRS	64,408	34.66	32,365
Huzurabad	Padi Kaushik Reddy	BRS	80,333	38.38	Etela Rajender	BJP	63,460	30.32	16,873
Husnabad (SC)	Ponnam Prabhakar	INC	1,00,955	48.84	Voditela Satish Kumar	BRS	81,611	39.48	19,344
Siddipet	Thanneeru Harish Rao	BRS	1,05,514	58.17	Pujala Hari Krishna	INC	23,206	12.79	82,308
Medak	Mynampally Rohith	INC	87,126	46.63	Padma Devender Reddy	BRS	76,969	41.19	10,157
Narayankhed	Patlolla Sanjeeva Reddy	INC	91,373	47.09	Mahareddy Bhupal Reddy	BRS	84,826	43.72	6,547
Andole (SC)	C. Damodar Raja Narasimha	INC	1,14,147	53.65	Chanti Karanthi Kiran	BRS	85,954	40.4	28,193
Narsapur	Vakiti Sunitha Laxma Reddy	BRS	88,410	44.64	Aavula Raji Reddy	INC	79,555	40.17	8,855
Zahirabad (SC)	Koninty Manik Rao	BRS	97,205	46.49	A. Chandrasekhar Rao	INC	84,415	40.37	12,790

Constituency Name	Winner				Runner Up				Margin
	Candidate	Party	Votes	%	Candidate	Party	Votes	%	
Sangareddy	Chinta Prabhakar	BRS	83.112	44.32	Jagga Reddy	INC	74,895	39.94	8,217
Patancheru	Gudem Mahipal Reddy	BRS	1,05,387	38.06	Kata Srinivas Goud	INC	98,296	35.5	7,091
Dubbak	Kotha Prabhakar Reddy	BRS	97.879	56.01	Raghunandan Rao	BJP	44,366	25.39	53,513
Gajwel	K Chandrashekar Rao	BRS	1,11,684	48.05	Etela Rajender	BJP	66,653	28.68	45,031
Medchal	Chamakura Malla Reddy	BRS	1,86,017	46.44	Thotakura Vajresh Yadav	INC	1,52,598	38.1	33,419
Malkajgiri	Marri Rajashekar Reddy	BRS	1,25,049	47.12	Mynampally Hanumanth Rao	INC	75,519	28.45	49,530
Quthbullapur	K. P. Vivekanand	BRS	1,87,999	46.8	Kuna Srisailam Goud	BJP	1,02,423	25.5	85,576
Kukatpally	Madhavaram Krishna Rao	BRS	1,35,636	54.08	Bandi Ramesh	INC	65,248	26.02	70,387
Uppal	Bandari Lakshma Reddy	BRS	1,32,927	48.33	Mandumula Parameshwar Reddy	INC	83,897	30.51	49,030
Ibrahimpatnam	Malreddy Ranga Reddy	INC	1,26,506	50.92	Manchireddy Kishan Reddy	BRS	89,806	36.14	36,700
L. B. Nagar	Devireddy Sudhir Reddy	BRS	1,11,380	37.74	Sama Ranga Reddy	BJP	89,075	30.18	22,305
Maheshwaram	Sabitha Indra Reddy	BRS	1,25,578	40.99	Andela Sriramulu Yadav	BJP	99,391	32.45	26,187
Rajendranagar	T. Prakash Goud	BRS	1,21,734	37.09	Thokala Srinivas Reddy	BJP	89,638	27.31	32,096
Serilingampally	Arekapudi Gandhi	BRS	1,57,332	43.97	Jagadeeswar Goud	INC	1,10,780	30.96	46,552
Chevella (SC)	Kale Yadaiah	BRS	76,218	38.73	Beem Bharath Pamena	INC	75,950	38.59	268
Pargi	Tammannagari Ram Mohan Reddy	INC	98,536	48.93	K. Mahesh Reddy	BRS	74,523	37.01	24,013
Vicarabad (SC)	Gaddam Prasad Kumar	INC	86,885	49.85	Dr.Methuku Anand	BRS	73,992	42.46	12,893
Tandur	B.Manohar Reddy	INC	84,662	48.32	Pilot Rohith Reddy	BRS	78,079	44.56	6,583
Musheerabad	Muta Gopal	BRS	75,207	49.07	Anjan Kumar Yadav	INC	37,410	24.41	37,797
Malakpet	Ahmed Bin Abdullah Balala	AIMIM	55,805	42.27	Shaik Akbar	INC	29,699	22.5	26,106

Constituency Name	Winner				Runner Up				Margin
	Candidate	Party	Votes	%	Candidate	Party	Votes	%	
Amberpet	Kaleru Venkatesh	BRS	74,416	50.8	Chenaboyanna Krishna Yadav	BJP	49,879	34.05	24,537
Khairatabad	Danam Nagender	BRS	67,368	43.48	P.Vijaya Reddy	INC	45,358	29.28	22,010
Jubilee Hills	Maganti Gopinath	BRS	80,549	43.94	Mohammed Azharuddin	INC	64,212	35.03	16,337
Sanathnagar	Talasani Srinivas Yadav	BRS	72,557	56.57	Marri Shashidhar Reddy	BJP	30,730	23.96	41,827
Nampally	Mohammad Majid Hussain	AIMIM	62,185	40.83	Mohammed Feroz Khan	INC	60,148	39.49	2,037
Karwan	Kausar Mohiuddin	AIMIM	83,388	47.42	Amar Singh	BJP	41,402	23.55	41,986
Goshamahal	T. Raja Singh	BJP	80,182	54.08	Nand Kishore Vyas	BRS	58,725	39.61	21,457
Charminar	Mir Zulfeqar Ali	AIMIM	49,103	50.05	Megha Rani Agarwal	BJP	26,250	26.76	22,853
Chandrayangutta	Akbaruddin Owaisi	AIMIM	99,776	64.89	Muppi Seetharam Reddy		BRS	18,116	11.78 81,660
Yakutpura	Jaffer Hussain	AIMIM	46,153	32.86	Amjed Ullah Khan	MBT	45,275	32.24	878
Bahadurpura	Mohammed Mubeen	AIMIM	89,451	62.24	Mir Inayath Ali Baqri	BRS	22,426	15.6	67,025
Secunderabad	T. Padma Rao Goud	BRS	78,223	55.42	Adam Santosh Kumar	INC	32,983	23.37	45,240
Secunderabad Cantt. (SC)	G. Lasya Nanditha	BRS	59,057	47.43	Sri Ganesh Narayan	BJP	41,888	33.64	17,169
Kodangal	Anumula Revanth Reddy	INC	1,07,429	55.05	Patnam Narender Reddy	BRS	74,897	38.38	32,532
Narayanpet	Chittem Parinika Reddy	INC	84,708	46.31	S.Rajender Reddy	BRS	76,757	41.97	7,951
Mahbubnagar	Yennam Srinivas Reddy	INC	87,227	48.04	V. Srinivas Goud	BRS	64, 489	37.72	18,738
Jadcherla	Janampalli Anirudh Reddy	INC	90,865	50.3	Charlakola Laxma Rreddy	BRS	75,694	41.9	15,171
Devarkadra	Gavinolla Madhu sudan Reddy	INC	88,551	45.31	Alla Venkateswar Reddy	BRS	87,159	44.6	1,392
Makthal	Vakiti Srihari	INC	74,917	39.88	Chittem Ram Mohan Reddy	BRS	57,392	30.55	17,525

Constituency Name	Winner				Runner Up				Margin
	Candidate	Party	Votes	%	Candidate	Party	Votes	%	
Wanaparthy	Tudi Megha Reddy	INC	1,07,115	50.25	Singireddy Niranjan Reddy	BRS	81,795	38.37	25,320
Gadwal	Bandla Krishna Mohan Reddy	BRS	94,097	43.79	Saritha Thirupathaiah	INC	87,061	40.52	7,036
Alampur (SC)	Vijayudu	BRS	1,04,060	52.88	S. A. Sampath Kumar	INC	73,487	37.34	30,573
Nagarkurnool	Kuchkulla Rajesh Reddy	INC	87,161	47.21	Marri Janardhan Reddy	BRS	81,913	44.37	5,248
Achampet (SC)	Chikkudu Vamshi Krishna	INC	1,15,337	58.96	Guvvala Balaraju	BRS	66,011	33.74	49,326
Kalwakurthy	Kasireddy Narayan Reddy	INC	75,858	37.41	Talloju Achary	BJP	70,448	34.75	5,410
Shadnagar	K. Shankaraiah	INC	77,817	39.79	Yelganamoni Anjaiah	BRS	70,689	36.15	7,128
Kollapur	Jupally Krishna Rao	INC	93,609	48.7	Beeram Harsha Vardhan Reddy	BRS	63,678	33.13	29,931
Devarakonda (ST)	Nenavath Balu Naik	INC	1,11,344	52.06	Ravindra Kumar Ramavath	BRS	81,323	38.02	30,021
Nagarjuna Sagar	Kunduru Jayaveer Reddy	INC	1,19,831	59.3	Nomula Bhagath Kumar	BRS	63,982	31.66	44,849
Miryalaguda	Bathula Laxma Reddy	INC	1,14,462	59.08	Nallamothu Bhaskar Rao	BRS	65,680	33.9	48,782
Huzurnagar	Nalamada Uttam Kumar Reddy	INC	1,16,707	54.21	Shanampudi Saidi Reddy	BRS	71,819	33.36	44,888
Kodad	Nalamada Padmavathi Reddy	INC	1,25,783	60.19	Bollam Mallaiah Yadav	BRS	67,611	32.35	58,172
Suryapet	Guntakandla Jagadish Reddy	BRS	75,143	36.36	Damodar Reddy Ramreddy	INC	70,537	34.13	4,606
Nalgonda	Komatireddy Venkat Reddy	INC	1,07,405	52.64	Kancharla. Bhupal Reddy	BRS	53,073	26.01	54,332
Munugode	Komatireddy Raj Gopal Reddy	INC	1,19,624	51.21	Kusukuntla Prabhakar Reddy	BRS	79,034	33.83	40,590

Constituency Name	Winner				Runner Up				Margin
	Candidate	Party	Votes	%	Candidate	Party	Votes	%	
Bhongir	Kumbam Anil Kumar Reddy	INC	1,02,742	52.4	Pailla Shekar Reddy	BRS	76,541	39.04	26,201
Nakrekal (SC)	Vemula Veeresham	INC	1,33,540	60.97	Chirumarthy Lingaiah	BRS	64,701	29.54	68,839
Thungathurthi (SC)	Mandula Samual	INC	1,29,535	57.53	Gadari Kishore	BRS	78,441	34.84	51,094
Alair	Beerla Ilaiah	INC	1,22,140	57.41	Gongidi Sunitha	BRS	72,504	34.08	49,636
Jangaon	Palla Rajeshwar Reddy	BRS	98,975	48.61	Kommuri Pratap Reddy	INC	83,192	40.86	15,783
Ghanpur (Station) (SC)	Kadiyam Srihari	BRS	1,01,696	47.13	Singhapuram Indira	INC	93,917	43.53	7,779
Palakurthi	Mamidala Yashaswini Reddy	INC	1,26,848	57.62	Errabelli Dayakar Rao	BRS	79,214	35.98	47,634
Dornakal (ST)	Jatoth Ram Chander Naik	INC	1,15,587	60.01	Dharamsoth Redya Naik	BRS	62,456	32.42	53,131
Mahabubabad (ST)	Murali Naik Bhukya	INC	1,16,644	55.46	Banoth Shankar Naik	BRS	66,473	31.6	50,171
Narsampet	Donthi Madhava Reddy	INC	1,04,185	50.73	Peddi Sudarshan Reddy	BRS	85,296	41.53	18,889
Parkal	Revuri Prakash Reddy	INC	72,573	38.46	Challa. Dharma Reddy.	BRS	64,632	34.25	7,941
Warangal West	Naini Rajender Reddy	INC	72,649	43.5	Dasyam Vinay Bhasker	BRS	57,318	34.32	15,331
Warangal East	Konda Surekha	INC	67,757	39.47	Errabelli Pradeep Kumar Rao	BJP	52,105	30.35	15,652
Waradhanapet (SC)	K. R. Nagaraj	INC	1,06,696	48.77	Aroori Ramesh	BRS	87,238	39.88	19,458
Bhupalpalle	Gandra Satyanarayana Rao	INC	1,23,116	54.55	Gandra Venkata Ramana Reddy	BRS	70,417	31.2	52,699
Mulug (ST)	Seethakka	INC	1,02,267	54.52	Bade Nagajyothi	BRS	68,567	36.55	33,700
Pinapaka (ST)	Payam Venkateswarlu	INC	90,510	56.61	Kantha Rao Rega	BRS	56,004	35.03	34,506

Winner				Runner Up				Margin
Candidate	Party	Votes	%	Candidate	Party	Votes	%	
Koram Kanakaiah	INC	1,09,171	61.22	Banoth Hari Priya	BRS	51,862	29.08	57,309
Tummala Nageswara Rao	INC	1,36,016	57.58	Puvvada Ajay Kumar	BRS	86,635	36.67	49,381
Ponguleti Srinivasa Reddy	INC	1,27,820	58.94	Kandala Upender Reddy	BRS	71,170	32.82	56,650
Mallu Bhatti Vikramarka	INC	1,08,970	55.49	Lingala Kamal Raju	BRS	73,518	37.44	35,452
Ramdas Maloth	INC	93,913	55.44	Banoth Madanlal	BRS	60,868	35.93	33,045
Matta Raga mayee	INC	1,11,245	51.66	Sandra Venkata Veeraiah	BRS	91,805	42.63	19,440
Kunamneni Sambasiva Rao	CPI	80,336	42.75	Jalagam Venkat Rao	AIFB	53,789	28.62	26,547
Jare Adinara yana	INC	74,993	55.05	Mecha Nageswara Rao	BRS	46,088	33.83	28,905
Tellam Venkata Rao	BRS	53,252	45.08	Podem Veeraiah	INC	47,533	40.24	5,719

Who's who

Name	Department
Anumula Revanth Reddy Chief Minister	Municipal Administration and Urban Development; General Administration, Law & Order and all other unallocated portfolios
Batti Vikramarka Mallu Deputy Chief Minister	Finance & Planning, Energy
Nalamada Uttam Kumar Reddy	Irrigation & CAD; Food & Civil Supplies
Damodar Rajanarasimha	Health, Medical & Family Welfare, Science and Technology
Komatireddy Venkat Reddy	Roads & Buildings, Cinematography
Duddilla Sridhar Babu	Information Technology, Electronics & Communications; Industries & Commerce and Legislative Affairs
Ponguleti Srinivas Reddy	Revenue and Housing, Information & Public Relations
Ponnam Prabhakar	Transport; BC Welfare
Konda Surekha	Environment & Forests, Endowment
Dr. Dansari Anasuya Seethakka	Panchayat Raj & Rural Development (including Rural Water Supply), Women & Child Welfare
Tummala Nageswara Rao	Agriculture, Marketing, Co-operation, and Handlooms & Textiles
Jupally Krishna Rao	Prohibition & Excise; Tourism & Culture and Archaeology

Postscript

Democracy is a form of government in which power is vested in the hands of the people, either directly or through elected representatives. It is a system where citizens can participate in decision-making, express their opinions, and choose their leaders. Democracy is often contrasted with other forms of government, such as autocracy (rule by a single individual), oligarchy (rule by a small group), and monarchy (rule by a hereditary monarch). While democracy is widely regarded as a system that promotes individual freedoms and political stability, it also faces challenges such as voter apathy, political polarisation, and the potential for manipulation. The effectiveness of a democratic system depends on the active and informed participation of its citizens.

The importance of voters in a democracy cannot be overstated or understated. Voters play a crucial role in shaping the direction of a democratic society, and their participation is fundamental to the functioning of a democratic system. We all know that voting allows citizens to choose representatives to decide on their behalf. This ensures that the government reflects the people's will and is accountable to them. Regular elections ensure that leaders are responsible to the people, reducing the risk of tyranny.

No politician or party should consider themselves indispensable in a democracy, a trait that was possibly visible before the elections among the then-ruling party leaders. Elected representatives are accountable to the voters, and the day citizens are dissatisfied with the performance of their representatives, they can express their displeasure by voting them out in the next election. Through voting, citizens usually contribute to social change by supporting candidates and policies that align with their values and aspirations. This can lead to the advancement of social justice, equality, and other important societal goals.

In summary, voters play a pivotal role as the bedrock of a thriving democracy, imparting crucial elements of legitimacy, representation, and accountability to the system. Their active involvement through the act of voting is not only fundamental but also indispensable for fostering the robust health and sustained success of democratic societies. By exercising their right to vote, citizens contribute significantly to the dynamic interplay of ideas and values, thereby shaping the collective trajectory of their nation and ensuring that the democratic fabric remains resilient and responsive to the diverse needs of its people.

Elections, as depicted in these pages, are not mere exercises in counting votes; they embody collective will, the manifestation of citizens' aspirations, and the instrument through which power is peacefully transferred.

Writing this book, Resonance of Democracy, has been a journey of passion for me, but it truly comes to life when readers like you engage with its ideas and perspectives. Your decision to invest your time and intellect in this book is humbling and inspiring. Politics is a complex and ever-evolving subject, and I aimed to provide readers with a nuanced understanding that encourages thoughtful reflection and dialogue. Your decision to accompany me on this journey is a testament to your curiosity to possibly know a new and different dimension to the Telangana State Assembly elections 2023. My core objective in writing this book was to make this a reference point to the happenings of this time for the times ahead.

This book underscores the significance of active citizenry and the role each individual plays in shaping the destiny of a democratic nation. The book invites readers to reflect on the ideals that underpin the electoral process and to consider the implications of the choices made by the electorate.

Through this book, I attempted to navigate the intricacies of the political campaigns, the candidates, and the issues that captured the attention of the electorate of Telangana State. Using data collated through the research, interactions, personal understanding, and insightful analysis of experts, I tried to provide a nuanced understanding of the challenges faced by the state, the aspirations of its people, and the evolving nature of the political dynamics of the youngest state. In the process of writing this book, I passed through numerous emotions. This journey through democracy and elections possibly made me understand the role and "enormous power" voters hold. I strongly feel that people who are made to feel like emperors during the election season should realise the responsibilities that come with the privilege of casting a vote and the imperative to remain engaged beyond the polling booth.

In essence, this book is not just a collection of narratives and analyses but an invitation to join the ongoing narrative of democracy. As the narrative draws to a close, readers are left to interpret for themselves what the future holds for Telangana and the vibrancy of democracy in the state, possibly providing an understanding of the intricate web of factors that influence political outcomes. This book is not only a historical account of the 2023 Telangana State Assembly elections but also a record of the happenings in the State and an exploration of the enduring resonance of democratic values in the heart of the Indian political landscape.

I sincerely hope that 'Resonance of Democracy' has met your expectations, sparking new ideas or offering fresh perspectives on the political landscape of Telangana. Your feedback and insights are invaluable to me as they contribute to the ongoing conversation essential in our society. If there are specific aspects of the book that resonated with you or if you have any thoughts you'd like to share, I would be genuinely interested in hearing from you. Your feedback will help me grow as a writer and shape my future endeavours. Once again, thank you for being an essential part of the readership community. Your support means a lot to me, and I am grateful for the opportunity to share my thoughts and ideas with individuals who appreciate the importance of thoughtful political discourse.

Acknowledgements

In the era of shorts and reels, book reading has become an almost dying habit, let alone writing a book. It requires discipline, dedication, and perseverance to streamline one's thoughts and pen them down systematically. For this reason, inspiration and encouragement are of utmost importance, which one gets from many quarters. Acknowledgement is but a mere token of expression of thanks to all those who made this gigantic effort possible.

Apart from being an inspiration for writing this book, these individuals have a role in shaping the past two decades of my life, which is filled with many beautiful memories. I also have a long list of friends and well-wishers whose contributions to my life I have not mentioned here but will remain in my heart forever.

Sreekar Reddy

He is "my brother" from "another mother". He was the first one to believe that I could write a book. Sreekar is the first person to whom I must express my deepest gratitude for his unwavering encouragement and belief in my abilities, which catalysed this writing journey. It was a coincidence that he was by my side when the thought of writing this book germinated in my mind, though I had not mentioned it to him earlier. A friend for more than two decades and a relationship that hopefully will last much longer, Sreekar Reddy's steadfast support, insightful feedback, and enthusiasm towards work and profession have been invaluable throughout my career.

Nitin Tanksale

He is a friend who is "dear to my heart". He is the only reason I can write this book. Since we met, Nitin has been a pillar of support, and this book is as much his as mine. I am profoundly thankful for his constant encouragement in all matters. Nitin thought I should work with him, travel with him, meet prominent politicians, and think along with him. Despite my ignorance of political and election communications, Nitin believed in my insight and ability. Without his help, I could not have gained such a deep understanding of politics and elections. I would not have written this book.

Over the years, I have seen Nitin, one of India's best political campaign strategists, design and develop some of the most brilliant and highly effective poll strategies, which yielded the best results. His deep understanding of Indian politics and his command over Hindi make interacting with Nitin the best and most enriching experience. I am at a loss of words to thank Nitin enough for his role in my life.

Srikanth Lingidi

Not everyone you meet casually and for a brief while will change your life for good. However, a chance meeting with Srikanth garu had a huge positive impact on my life. Though we belong to two different worlds, it was a miracle how these worlds converged to bring us close to each other. Srikanth has remained a pillar of strength since he learned about my plans to write a book on Telangana elections. He was a constant source of support and encouragement for me, without which I could not have completed this book.

Rajesh 'Sir'

Rajesh Gurram was my first boss. He gave me my first job and provided multiple opportunities to grow in my career. I fondly refer to him as "My Boss" whenever I refer to him. He has been instrumental in shaping my life on many fronts. During the formative years of my career as a public relations professional, despite his busy work schedule, Rajesh 'Sir' ensured he spoke to me for long hours and discussed nuances, which helped me professionally and personally. His contribution towards shaping me is unparalleled. Rajesh 'Sir' gave me many opportunities to emerge as a better professional, though I did not make the best use of them. There have been multiple instances when I pushed him into rough weather, but he has always bailed me out of difficult situations. I will be forever thankful to him for all his support and advice.

Pavan Nanduri

Some people around you make your life easy. Pavan Nanduri, whom I admiringly call "Rafi" for his singing skills and his liking for legendary singer Mohammad Rafi, is one such individual. I took him into the team in September 2022, and since then, he has been a pillar of strength for us. He shared my workload, which helped me to stay focused on writing this book. Thank you, Pavan!

Umamaheshwar S.

I initially knew Mahesh only as a journalist. Our association spans over two decades and has been an enriching experience for me. He is the only author (of *Roving Eyes - Love, Lust, and Battles of Indian Royalty*) I know personally. My interest in writing a book started after seeing Mahesh publish his work. I am a huge fan of Mahesh's knowledge of Indian history, business, and politics. An award-winning journalist (a winner of the Shriram Sanlam Award for Financial Journalism in 2016), Mahesh is the only one who came to mind when I decided to write a book and wanted him to edit my work. I know it would have been a painstaking effort for him to edit this book, and I will be forever thankful to him.

Prof. Karnam Narender

"Gurur Brahma Gurur Vishnu Gurur Devo Maheshwaraha
Guru Saakshaat Parabrahma Tasmai Sri Gurave Namaha"

My guru, Prof. Karnam Narender, is one of the most important people in my journey. An ever-approachable for his wards, "Narender Sir" (as I call him) is known for his flair and is possibly the best teacher one can have. Irrespective of a student's awkward or indifferent attitude towards him, Narender Sir has always welcomed his wards with a smile and grace. I had personally experienced Narender Sir's love and affection in what would possibly be the most difficult phase of his career at Osmania University.

His friendly demeanour and welcoming attitude make him an affable person. It's only by luck that one meets such a teacher who is always willing to walk the difficult miles with his students.

Sir, I know this work might not meet your expectations, and you would wish more from your wards. I am sure you will bless this student of yours the best in life. Thank you very much, sir, for always being there for me.

Bibliography

This book is made of my personal experiences and observations that I had in the run-up to and during the Telangana State Assembly elections 2023. In addition to the understanding I developed over the past two decades about this region and its politics, I gathered a lot of insights about its political landscape in the last two years through watching and reading about the unfolding political developments.

While it is difficult to reproduce an exhaustive list of all my sources, the following are links to some of my sources that I referred to while authoring this book.

https://en.wikipedia.org/wiki/2023_Telangana_Legislative_Assembly_election#:~:text=The%20votes%20were%20counted%20and,declared%20on%203%20December%202023.&text=The%20Indian%20National%20Congress%20(INC,BRS)'s%2039%20seats

https://en.wikipedia.org/wiki/Telangana_Legislative_Assembly

https://www.ndtv.com/india-news/telangana-election-results-2023-live-updates-counting-of-votes-to-begin-at-8-am-4623658

https://www.thehindu.com/elections/telangana-assembly/telangana-assembly-election-results-2023-congress-takes-over-telangana-from-bharat-rashtra-samithi/article67602343.ece

https://www.thehindu.com/elections/telangana-assembly/telangana-assembly-election-results-2023-congress-takes-over-telangana-from-bharat-rashtra-samithi/article67602343.ece

https://timesofindia.indiatimes.com/india/telangana-election-results-2023-live-updates-ts-assembly-elections-counting-bjp-congress-brs/live-blog/105685361.cms

https://www.ndtv.com/india-news/telangana-election-results-2023-live-updates-counting-of-votes-to-begin-at-8-am-4623658
https://www.thehindu.com/elections/telangana-assembly/revanth-reddy-is-the-new-chief-minister-of telangana/article67608096.ece#:~:text=Ending%20two%20days%20of%20suspense,of%20office%20on%20December%207.

https://www.thehindu.com/news/national/telangana/revanth-reddy-govt-heralding-a-shift-in-policy-pragathi-bhavan-barricades-torndown/article67614078.ece#:~:text=The%20barricaded%20pathway%20leading%20to,vehicular%20traffic%20for%20several%20years.

https://www.deccanchronicle.com/nation/politics/301223/removing-barricades-at-pragathi-bhavan-a-brave-move-cpi.html

https://www.thehindubusinessline.com/news/congress-clinches-telangana-kcr-defeated-at-kamareddy/article67601603.ece

https://www.telegraphindia.com/india/bharatiya-janata-partys-k-venkata-ramana-reddy-emerges-as-giant-slayer-defeats-k-chandrasekhar-rao-revanth-reddy-in-kamareddy/cid/1984318

https://indianexpress.com/article/political-pulse/telangana-bjp-double-giant-killer-katipally-venkata-ramana-reddy-9052819/

https://thesouthfirst.com/telangana/dual-giant-slayer-of-kamareddy-meet-bjps-k-venkata-ramana-reddy-who-beat-kcr-revanth-reddy/

https://indianexpress.com/article/cities/hyderabad/telangana-assembly-election-results-2023-full-list-of-winners-9050593/

https://www.thehindubusinessline.com/news/telangana-rajasthan-madhya-pradesh-chhattisgarh-assembly-election-results-2023-highlights/article67599145.ece

https://timesofindia.indiatimes.com/elections/assembly-elections/telangana/videos/congress-will-fulfill-promises-made-to-telangana-says-revanth-reddy-after-historic-win/videoshow/105705782.cms

https://www.thehindu.com/news/national/telangana/revanth-reddy-alleges-potential-bjp-brs-alliance-promises-swift-implementation-of-poll-promises/article67777551.ece
https://www.ndtv.com/india-news/telangana-election-result-2023-will-fulfill-all-promises-says-revanth-reddy-after-telangana-win-4630507

https://www.livemint.com/politics/news/telangana-cm-revanth-reddy-fulfills-first-poll-promise-gets-iron-barricades-removed-from-office-premises-watch-11701940233656.html

https://www.newstap.in/telangana/revanth-reddy-promises-4-women-ministers-in-telangana-congress-cabinet-1504462

https://www.deccanchronicle.com/nation/politics/031223/telangana-election-results-revanth-reddy-invites-kcr-to-join-hands-in.html

https://news.abplive.com/elections/telangana-results-2023-congress-revival-in-kcr-state-revanth-reddy-new-congress-hero-challenges-ahead-kcr-loss-abpp-1647532 https://www.businesstoday.in/latest/politics/story/new-telangana-cm-revanth-reddy-approves-congress-6-poll-guarantees-on-day-1-408590-2023-12-07

https://www.hindustantimes.com/india-news/revanth-reddy-faces-internal-external-challenges-as-he-takes-over-as-telangana-cm-101701935322009.html

https://www.ndtv.com/telangana-news/minutes-after-taking-oath-telangana-chief-minister-revanth-reddy-fulfills-a-key-poll-promise-4642225

https://www.livemint.com/elections/telangana-election-2023-congress-manifesto-six-guarantees-free-bus-travel-women-free-electricity-pension-farmers-11700211790990.html

https://indianexpress.com/article/india/revanth-reddy-takes-oath-as-telangana-cm-clears-congs-6-guarantees-in-1st-step-9059073/

https://news.abplive.com/elections/telangana-elections-congress-chief-revanth-reddy-mocks-bjp-over-poll-manifesto-1643811

https://www.thehindu.com/news/national/telangana/congress-created-new-india-but-kcr-and-modi-are-enjoying-the-fruits-says-revanth-reddy/article67197037.ece

https://frontline.thehindu.com/politics/congress-defeats-brs-with-aggressive-campaign-in-telangana/article67617727.ece
https://www.deccanherald.com/opinion/telangana-congress-victory-a-triumph-of-strategic-campaigning-civil-society-activism-2795035

https://www.livemint.com/elections/assembly-elections/telangana-assembly-elections-2023-rahul-and-priyanka-to-kick-off-congress-poll-campaign-on-october-18-11697167150173.html https://www.indiatoday.in/elections/telangana-assembly-polls-2023/story/telangana-election-2023-congress-indira-gandhi-indi-ramma-rajyam-poll-campaign-kcr-2468793-2023-11-29

https://timesofindia.indiatimes.com/elections/assembly-elections/telangana/videos/telangana-polls-2023-telangana-congress-unleashes-bye-bye-kcr-campaign-in-a-fiery-political-move/videoshow/104970019.cms

https://indianexpress.com/article/political-pulse/telangana-election-results-aimim-old-hyderabad-9052508/

https://www.thequint.com/elections/telangana-election/aimim-owaisi-hyderabad-brs-congress-revanth-reddy-yakutpura-karwan

https://www.hindustantimes.com/india-news/elections-results-bjp-ahead-of-asaduddin-owaisis-aimim-in-telangana-101701592863122.html

https://www.thehindu.com/news/national/telangana/aimim-clings-on-to-its-seven-assembly-seats/article67602395.ece

https://www.livemint.com/elections/assembly-elections/assembly-elections-2023-live-updates-telangana-mp-trs-rahul-gandhi-congress-kcr-pm-modi-brs-kharge-legislative-assembly-11701054860136.html

https://www.thehindu.com/elections/telangana-assembly/winds-of-change-blowing-strongly-in-favour-of-bjp-in-telangana-says-pm-modi/article67573044.ece

https://www.livemint.com/elections/assembly-elections/election-results-amit-shah-thanks-telangana-for-support-even-as-bjp-loses-to-

congress-set-to-form-govt-in-3-states-117016042051 32.html

https://www.thehindu.com/elections/telangana-assembly/saddened-by-extent-of-corruption-in-telangana-pawan-kalyan/article67561722.ece

https://www.ndtv.com/india-news/telangana-assembly-election-2023-in-telangana-pm-modi-shares-stage-with-pawan-kalyan-4555799

https://www.moneycontrol.com/news/assembly-elections/telangana/bjp-pawan-kalyans-jana-sena-to-contest-telangana-assembly-polls-together-11668981.html

https://www.ndtv.com/india-news/pawan-kalyans-party-releases-names-of-8-candidates-for-telangana-assembly-polls-2023-4555501

https://timesofindia.indiatimes.com/elections/assembly-elections/telangana/news/all-8-candidates-of-pawan-kalyans-party-lose-deposit/articleshow/105710777.cms

https://www.thehindu.com/elections/telangana-assembly/pawan-kalyan-public-meeting-in-warangal/article67558805.ece

https://www.thehindu.com/elections/telangana-assembly/congress-did-not-implement-mandal-commission-report-says-mayawati-in-telangana/article67571131.ece

https://www.hindustantimes.com/cities/lucknow-news/mayawati-to-kickstart-bsp-s-telangana-election-campaign-101700588312356.html

https://en.themooknayak.com/politics/bsps-telangana-campaign-targets-political-giants-mayawati-and-rs-praveen-kumar-take-center-stage https://m.economictimes.com/news/elections/assembly-elections/telangana-assembly-elections/mayawati-launches-telangana-campaign-with-attack-on-congress-reminds-voters-mandal-was-under-v-p-singh/videoshow/105416656.cms

https://www.thehindu.com/elections/telangana-assembly/bjp-brs-combined-is-our-main-opposition-says-bsp-chief-rs-praveen-kumar/article67580356.ece

https://www.hindustantimes.com/cities/lucknow-news/bsp-draws-a-blank-in-madhya-pradesh-chhattisgarh-and-telangana-gets-two-seats-in-rajasthan-101701620740625.html
https://timesofindia.indiatimes.com/elections/assemblyelections/telangana/videos/ telangana-polls-2023-bsp-transgender-candidate-pushpithalaya-conducts-election-campaign-in-warangal/videoshow/105360608.cms

https://indianexpress.com/article/political-pulse/assembly-election-results-2023-tribals-dalits-bjp-bsp-9054939/

https://www.indiatoday.in/elections/telangana-assembly-polls-2023/video/telangana-assembly-elections-decoding-the-mood-of-the-youth-2458915-2023-11-06

https://www.moneycontrol.com/news/opinion/telangana-elections-2023-failure-to-create-adequate-jobs-troubles-kcr-11814611.html

https://indianexpress.com/article/opinion/editorials/in-telangana-and-rajasthan-the-youth-want-jobs-not-welfare-9035323/a

https://www.moneycontrol.com/news/assembly-elections/telangana/telangana-assembly-elections-2023-barrelakka-a-symbol-of-

resilience-will-she-be-peoples-choice-11837041.html

https://www.thehindu.com/news/national/telangana/slapped-with-a-case-for-spoof-video-telanganas-barrelakka-enters-poll-fray/article67521206.ece

https://www.indiatoday.in/elections/story/kollapur-assembly-election-results-2023-live-2470998-2023-12-03

http://www.outlookindia.com/national/meet-barrelakka-the-emerging-voice-of-unemployed-graduates-in-telangana-elections-news-333325

https://indianexpress.com/article/political-pulse/independent-buffalo-sister-has-a-bull-run-in-telangana-9038278/

https://telanganatoday.com/telangana-15-super-specialist-doctors-emerge-victorious-in-assembly-elections

https://www.indiatoday.in/elections/telangana-assembly-polls-2023/story/ysrtp-party-ys-sharmila-telangana-assembly-elections-not-contest-congress-brs-bjp-voting-2457615-2023-11-03

https://m.economictimes.com/news/elections/assembly-elections/telangana-assembly-elections/telangana-assembly-elections-sharmila-led-ysrtp-withdraws-from-poll-fray-to-support-congress/articleshow/104937766.cms

https://www.indiatvnews.com/telangana/news-telangana-assembly-poll-2023-sharmila-ysrtp-withdraws-assembly-election-contest-pledges-congress-support-latest-updates-2023-11-03-900997

https://thewire.in/politics/sharmilas-ysr-party-wont-contest-telangana-assembly-polls-offers-support-to-congress https://news.abplive.com/elections/telangana-elections-jagan-reddy-s-sister-ys-sharmila-s-big-move-i-stand-at-this-juncture-of-sacrifice-1640230

https://www.india.com/telangana/doctors-turn-netas-15-super-speciality-medics-becomes-mla-after-big-win-in-telangana-assembly-elections-2023-6566467/

https://timesofindia.indiatimes.com/city/hyderabad/docs-turn-netas-15-to-enter-house/articleshow/105739813.cms

https://www.thehindu.com/news/national/telangana/triumph-of-medicos-in-telangana-polls-sparks-calls-for-doctor-led-health-department/article67607470.ece

https://www.hindustantimes.com/india-news/telangana-assembly-elections-results-2023-live-updates-winning-candidates-full-list-how-many-seats-brs-congress-bjp-aimi-101701566532305.html

https://www.thehindu.com/elections/telangana-assembly/telangana-assembly-elections-2023-ai-connect-to-voters/article67566146.ece

https://www.ndtv.com/india-news/telangana-assembly-elections-all-you-need-to-know-4626244

https://thesouthfirst.com/news/techie-turned-independent-candidate-akarsh-sriramoju-envisages-a-samagra-serlingampally/

https://thewire.in/politics/telangana-bharat-rashtra-samithi-congress-kcr

https://www.sakshipost.com/news/telangana/techies-complain-it-firms-denying-holiday-polling-day-251683 https://www.deccanchronicle.com/nation/in-other-news/261123/no-off-for-voting-client-needs-come-first-say-companies.html

https://timesofindia.indiatimes.com/city/hyderabad/no-holiday-on-poll-day-irks-hyd-techies-latest-news/articleshow/105641387.cms

https://timesofindia.indiatimes.com/city/hyderabad/brs-won-most-seats-where-it-replaced-its-sitting-mlas/articleshow/105739020.cms

https://indianexpress.com/article/political-pulse/brs-holds-onto-hyderabad-urban-base-congress-draws-a-blank-9053237/

https://timesofindia.indiatimes.com/city/hyderabad/greater-hyd-minor-consolation-for-brs/articleshow/105711429.cms

https://www.businesstoday.in/latest/politics/story/telangana-assembly-election-results-two-it-hubs-hyderabad-and-bengaluru-under-congress-control-now-say-netizens-408025-2023-12-03

https://www.indiatoday.in/india-today-insight/story/how-greater-hyderabad-bucked-trend-gave-kcrs-party-a-vote-of-confidence-2471872-2023-12-04

https://www.deccanchronicle.com/nation/politics/031223/hyderabad-brs-congress-assembly-election-results.html

https://www.etvbharat.com/english/state/telangana/telangana-assembly-elections-2023/na20231203203147255255059

https://www.thenewsminute.com/telangana/brs-losses-congress-gains-how-telangana-voted-in-2023

https://www.livemint.com/elections/assembly-elections/telangana-assembly-election-result-2023-brs-leader-ktr-concedes-defeat-says-not-

saddened-surely-disappointed-11701597418925.html

https://timesofindia.indiatimes.com/elections/assembly-elections/telangana/videos/telangana-elections-2023-no-difference-between-ktr-and-rahul-gandhi-union-minister-g-kishan-reddy/videoshow/105269243.cms

https://www.ndtv.com/india-news/telangana-assembly-elections-2023-you-have-violated-poll-body-issues-notice-to-telangana-minister-kt-rama-rao-4606421

https://www.ndtv.com/india-news/telangana-assembly-elections-2023-richest-telangana-candidate-worth-rs-227-crore-poorest-has-rs-46-lakh-4614048

https://www.hindustantimes.com/india-news/brs-concedes-defeat-in-telangana-ktr-rao-congratulates-congress-101701596861096.html

https://www.hindustantimes.com/trending/girl-asks-ktr-mama-to-bring-disneyland-to-hyderabad-heres-what-the-minister-said-101701231594952.html

https://timesofindia.indiatimes.com/city/hyderabad/itminister-trends-after-ktr-signs-off/articleshow/105739290.cms

https://www.thehindu.com/elections/telangana-assembly/ktr-the-man-to-go-for-brs-candidates-in-urban-areas/article67551425.ece
https://www.thehindu.com/news/national/telangana/ktr-retains-sircilla-seat/article67601760.ece
https://www.siasat.com/hyderabad-wisely-voted-for-brs-congress-deceived-rural-telangana-ktr-2970593/
https://news.abplive.com/elections/telangana-assembly-elections-kt-rama-rao-brs-says-play-cricket-with-azharuddin-congress-1643528

Other titles

Book design: T. Kishore Kumar

www.ingramcontent.com/pod-product-compliance
Lightning Source LLC
LaVergne TN
LVHW010546160826
845677LV00013B/3014

* 9 7 8 8 1 9 7 0 5 3 4 1 2 *